Preserving *Paradise*

Preserving *Paradise*

The Architectural Heritage and History of the Florida Keys

George Walter Born

THE History PRESS

Published by The History Press
Charleston, SC 29403
www.historypress.net

Cover image: Asa Tift built this unusual stone house shortly after the Civil War. Tift was from New England but sided with the South during the war. During the 1930s, writer Ernest Hemingway lived and worked in this house, which is now open to the public. *907 Whitehead Street. Courtesy of the History Department, May Hill Russell Library, Key West.*

First published 2006

Manufactured in the United States

ISBN 978.1.59629.152.2

Library of Congress Cataloging-in-Publication Data

Born, George Walter.
Preserving paradise : the architectural heritage and history of the Florida Keys / George Walter Born.
p. cm.
ISBN 978-1-59629-152-2 (alk. paper)
1. Architecture--Conservation and restoration--Florida--Florida Keys. 2. Historic preservation--Florida--Florida Keys. I. Title.
NA107.F6B67 2006
720.9759'41--dc22
2006019577

Though for no other cause, yet for this;
that posterity may know
we have not loosely through silence permitted things to pass away as in a dream…

Richard Hooker (1554?–1600)

Contents

Acknowledgements

I would like to thank the Historic Florida Keys Foundation for supporting my writing about historic preservation. I am especially grateful to Jack London, former executive director, who as a member of the editorial advisory board of the *Key West Citizen* first arranged for me to write for the newspaper and who, as my supervisor at the time, proofread much of my work.

Additional thanks go to *Key West Citizen* editors Sally Mahan and Tom Tuell and their staff: Terry Schmida, Ralph Morrow, Stacy Willits Rodriguez, Chris Tittel and Nancy Klingener. They have provided a forum for my writings—from 2001 to the present.

I would also like to express my gratitude to the staff at the Monroe County Library in Key West. Tom Hambright, as keeper of the local history collections, was of great assistance in providing historical and illustrative material. Additionally, Anne Rice deserves praise for spearheading the effort to digitize hundreds of historic photographs, some of which are reproduced here.

I would like to show my appreciation, too, for Jason Chasteen of The History Press, who unbeknownst to me had been reading my newspaper columns and who surprised me with a phone call that led to this volume. What a delight to be asked to compile a book that I had, in great measure, already written. I thank him for his interest in giving my work a wider audience. His unfailing enthusiasm for the project made it a joy.

Additionally, I would like to acknowledge and thank writer and friend Walter de Milly for his moral support, over the course of years, in countless dinner conversations.

Finally, I am very grateful to my parents for encouraging precision and clarity in both thinking and writing.

Preface

The Florida Keys are a unique laboratory for studying and practicing historic preservation, offering a large and diverse collection of architecture, a colorful tradition of settlement and immigration, a tropical climate alternately languid and violent and a hothouse economic environment stimulating redevelopment of historic areas. In this region, these themes are as ubiquitous as Key lime pie.

"All preservation is local," it has been famously remarked, paraphrasing former Speaker of the House Thomas P. O'Neil's quip on politics. Especially in the context of American preservation practice, a decentralized, grassroots approach is plainly evident in the Keys and in countless other communities across the country.

At the same time, historic preservation now has a history—and a substantial body of professional principles, extracted from decades of practice in a wide range of locales. Reconciling the interplay of historic preservation in the Florida Keys with these broader concepts from the field as a whole has been the challenge and delight of the author for over a decade. The essays that follow reflect this interplay of ideas.

Vernacular Architecture

An uncommon word describing things that are common, "vernacular" often appears in connection with language. The saying "in the vernacular" describes a local dialect or way of speaking.

Vernacular architecture is the traditional building of the common people at a particular time and place. Because of its humble origins, some have called it "architecture without architects."

The strictest definition focuses on the modest buildings of the pre-industrial age. Vernacular design emerged from traditional and practical solutions to functional concerns, rather than from academic or theoretical notions of what high-style architecture should look like. Indeed, the designer of a vernacular building was likely to be the occupant himself or a builder with no formal architectural training, although he certainly possessed a thorough knowledge of his craft.

Additionally, vernacular buildings went up without detailed architectural plans, as designs stayed close to tried and true patterns. Materials were typically close to nature and available locally, such as indigenous wood and stone. The building process called upon artisans trained by apprenticeships in a tradition of handcraftsmanship. The result is a fascinating patchwork of highly distinctive regional building traditions. Indeed, some of the most distinctive vernacular architecture sprung up in areas isolated from more mainstream currents of thought.

Examples include thatched cottages in the British Isles, grass huts in the South Seas, adobe buildings in the American Southwest, Cape Cod cottages in New England, Quaker farmhouses in Pennsylvania, log cabins in the American West and conch houses in the Keys.

Here that usually suggests small, wood-frame structures built on limestone piers with a front porch, double-hung windows and gable roof covered with shingles (now of metal but often originally of wood).

This archetypal image of vernacular architecture, however, does not always stand by itself, insulated as a category from other modes of building. Over time, two influences have gradually come to encroach on this definition.

First, knowledge of architectural styles became increasingly common. In earliest times, only the educated elite could afford to employ architects to create refined, high-style buildings. This left the vast majority of people to build simple structures based on indigenous materials and traditions. Yet over time, greater communication with urban centers, the wider circulation of books about "correct" architecture and increasing wealth gradually introduced many more people to academic ideas of building.

This new sophistication little by little smoothed out radically differing regional styles, although it did not eliminate them entirely. Buildings often showed connections to both their traditional, indigenous roots as well as the newer influences from abroad. One British architectural historian called this border between vernacular and high-style architecture the "polite threshold."

Many buildings in Key West fall on this threshold, eluding precise classification. Embodying the essential characteristics of our local vernacular building tradition—simple, wood-frame houses with front porches—they also display stylistic detailing, especially in the Classical Revival style. By mainland standards, these are obviously Key West houses, but from a Key West point of view, they show an awareness of mainland architectural ideas.

The second influence to impact traditional vernacular architecture was the Industrial Revolution, which gradually undermined traditions of handcraftsmanship. Yet ordinary people still needed small, affordable buildings. Reaching beyond local craft traditions, builders soon turned to a wide variety of available pattern books for design assistance. They also made use of manufactured building materials resulting from the new industrial modes of production.

Key West examples of industrial vernacular architecture include the many cigar makers' cottages built by manufacturers for workers. Additionally one occasionally sees small houses based on plans copied from pattern books or sold as kits from major mail order companies, such as Sears, Roebuck, and Company. These homes constituted the affordable housing of their day.

All told, Key West's survey of historic resources lists 2,227 vernacular buildings—out of a total of 2,580—encompassing the vast majority of our architectural heritage. These humble buildings form our own distinctive legacy, a Keys contribution to the varied vernacular architecture around the world.

Classical Revival Architecture

When Edgar Allen Poe wrote of "the glory that was Greece, and the grandeur that was Rome," he spoke for many nineteenth-century Americans who found inspiration in the cultural achievement of the ancient world. Indeed, a significant portion of Key West's architectural heritage speaks to this legacy.

This revival of things classical was nothing new. Western civilization has looked to antiquity for guidance for centuries: its attractiveness is irresistible.

Greek civilization, thriving in the fifth century BC, gave the world a highly refined and monumental architecture. Found particularly in its temples, such as the Parthenon in Athens, Classical Greek style features rows of columns, topped by capitals, supporting low-pitched gable roofs. Additionally, the Greeks laid the foundation for western democracy, philosophy and theater.

Their Roman successors, flourishing between the first century BC and the third century AD, adopted much of Greek culture wholesale while also making their own contributions. In architecture, the Romans developed the arch, the vault and the dome to great effect. In other fields, Rome developed a republican government, a sprawling empire, a significant body of law and a voluminous Latin literature.

Following the fall of Rome in the fifth century, the cultural organization and achievements of the classical Mediterranean world declined precipitously, though not irrevocably.

Ancient Roman ruins inspired a revival of earlier building practice during the Middle Ages, known as the Romanesque style, known for its use of massive masonry arches.

The Renaissance flowered from the fourteenth to sixteenth centuries, utilizing classical forms with great correctness and creativity to produce some of the masterpieces of world architecture.

By the late eighteenth and early nineteenth centuries, intense interest in the ancient world revived once again. Publications on archaeological discoveries in Greece reached much of the English-speaking world beginning in the 1760s. The United States formed its own government two decades later, inspired by Greek democracy and Roman republicanism. Americans also sympathized with those fighting in the Greek War for Independence in the 1820s. All of this fostered the Greek—or Classical—Revival style of architecture.

In major urban centers, virtual copies of Greek temples sprung up in stone, housing banks, libraries and government buildings. Houses, too, adopted this form, although usually in a much-simplified way. The use of wood-frame construction, for example, represents a significant departure from ancient models. Additionally, columns, which in antiquity were always round, often became square in latter-day variations. Capitals, too, were often simply made of moldings instead of Greek-style elaborate carvings. Finally, bright white paint found wide use, echoing the bleached marble of classical ruins. Many Key West houses embody these adaptations.

Ironically the idea of living in a building that looks like a Greek temple would have been foreign to Greeks themselves, whose houses looked completely different—very simple, one-story buildings arranged around a central courtyard. Taking up residence in a sacred building would have seemed like living in a church today.

Yet the gable- or temple-front house became a mainstay of American architecture by the mid-nineteenth century. Key West has many examples of them, such as the Peter Williams ("Donkey Milk") House at 613 Eaton Street, the Gideon Lowe House (formerly "Whispers") at 409 William Street and the Thompson House at 1029 Fleming Street.

The precise number of Classical Revival buildings here varies depending upon how strictly one applies stylistic criteria. In earlier decades, scholars routinely classified structures with any hint of classical form or detail as manifestations of the style, in order to claim a connection to mainstream architectural history. More recently, as vernacular architecture has become more widely appreciated, local interpretations of faraway urban styles have achieved a new respectability, allowing them to be recognized for what they are. Either way, "conch temples" of Key West are a significant part of our heritage, stretching back to the dawn of Western architecture twenty-five hundred years ago.

Gothic Revival Style

One might not expect to find a link between medieval Europe and nineteenth-century Key West; yet a small but significant portion of our surviving architectural heritage bears witness to just such a connection centuries and oceans apart.

By the mid-nineteenth century, the Greek Revival style began to see challenges to its supremacy, as builders and designers sought something new—or at least something new to them. They found it by turning to the architecture of the Middle Ages, a period that offered a radically different design vocabulary and a refreshing change of pace.

Andrew Jackson Downing, an American landscape architect and writer, became one of the most passionate spokesmen for reviving the Gothic style. In his prolific writings, he railed against the cold monotony of classical, white-painted, columned buildings yanked out of their native Mediterranean and transplanted to the shores of North America. Instead, he envisioned picturesque, cozy cottages ornamented with medieval motifs, nestled into the landscape and offering warm hospitality within.

Downing also published designs, one of which (from 1850's *The Architecture of County Houses*) may have served as the inspiration for a house in Key West. Local architect William Kerr may even have owned a copy of this book when he built his home at 410 Simonton Street, which sports such typically Gothic features as a central peaked gable, a low wraparound porch, a miniature balcony, elaborate scroll-sawn gingerbread and decorative gable trim known as bargeboards or verge boards. Indeed, the house is such a good example of its type, it seems likely that Kerr saw it as a signboard for his talents.

Another example stands at 520 Angela Street across from City Hall. Executed in wood rather than traditional English stone, these designs embody the American approach known as Carpenter Gothic.

Such charming cottages, though memorable, are few in number in Key West. By far the larger number of buildings in the Gothic Revival style are religious in nature. This trend reflects a different line of reasoning. While quaint houses employing this mode reflected a Victorian ideal of virtuous domesticity, soaring Gothic religious buildings embodied a rather different—and more public—display of piety.

In England, leaders of the Oxford Movement called for a revival of traditional ritual and liturgy, a trend that had architectural ramifications. Indeed, by the second quarter of the nineteenth century, a number of writers and thinkers felt it flatly inappropriate to build a Christian church in a "pagan" classical style. Instead they looked to the cathedrals and parish churches of the Middle Ages, reviving the use of stained glass windows, pointed arches, steeply pitched roofs, corner towers and fortress-like crenellated parapets.

A look at some of the religious buildings in Key West shows that this trend made itself felt here. From a tiny chapel (now in secular use) at the corner of Whitehead and Julia Streets to the imposing landmark of St. Paul's at Duval and Eaton Streets, the use of these Gothic Revival elements is marked. Other examples include the Cornish Memorial AME Zion Church on Whitehead Street, Trinity Presbyterian Church on Simonton Street and St. Peter's Episcopal Church on Center Street. Even the old synagogue (now Sarabeth's) at the corner of Simonton and Southard Streets with its Tudor-arched windows suggests that the Jewish community also embraced the Gothic Revival style.

The use of this mode in religious buildings continued through the 1920s—long after it had passed from fashion for houses. And even though the actual numbers of buildings employing it are not great, they are significant due to their size and symbolic importance in the community.

Queen Anne Style

When most people envision Victorian architecture, they probably picture the Queen Anne style. With corner turrets, elaborate gingerbread decoration and other whimsical trimmings, this mode is one of the most fanciful of those popular in the nineteenth century. It enjoyed notable prominence here in Key West in the 1880s and 1890s, when the Island City flourished as Florida's largest city and its wealthiest per capita.

The Queen Anne style originated in England, which until the twentieth century was the most important source for architectural ideas in the United States.

Like the advocates of the Gothic Revival style before them, the creators of the Queen Anne style rebelled against cold and rigid classicism. Architects such as Richard Norman Shaw looked back before the orderly architecture of the Georgian period (1714–1820), finding inspiration instead from the rambling, vernacular manner of earlier English building practice. Consequently, they named the new style for Queen Anne, a British monarch who reigned from 1702 to 1714.

But other eras influenced the style, too, dating back to the late sixteenth century. Indeed, the leaders of the new movement drew upon centuries of architectural history to evoke the warm, picturesque qualities of traditional English buildings.

Interestingly, because the advocates of the Queen Anne style were not rigidly obsessed with a literal, period-correct revival of an earlier manner, they wound up producing an original, inventive expression and a free interpretation that is a distinctive phenomenon in its own right.

One of the most significant characteristics of this style is asymmetry, a direct reaction to the ruthless symmetry of Georgian classicism. Irregular massing is also notable, as Queen Anne style buildings may look like they have been added to over the years, even when they were built of one piece. Additionally, turrets—either round or octagonal—and bay windows add visual interest to roofs and walls. Other features of the Queen Anne style include steeply pitched roofs with multiple gables and dormers; fanciful ornamentation such as gingerbread, spindles and metal cresting; tall chimneys; extensive, often asymmetrical porches; and the use of multiple siding materials (such as clapboards and patterned shingles) to produce a textured wall appearance.

Many of these elaborate features were made possible by advances in the Industrial Revolution, which gradually transformed the process of building in the nineteenth century. For example, the development of the balloon framing system, using standard milled lumber and cheap wire nails, made construction of elaborate forms and designs easier than ever. In addition, fancy decorative trim, such as gingerbread and spindles, became increasingly available as band saws and power lathes saw greater usage in lumberyards and mills.

The publication of pattern books hastened the spread of the Queen Anne style, enabling patrons and builders far from the original home of the movement to become familiar with its designs. Examples of this style in Key West include the Artist House, 534 Eaton Street, built for Thomas Osgood Otto after the 1886 fire; the Southernmost House, 1400 Duval Street, constructed for J. Vining and Florida Curry Harris at the turn of the last century; the George Bowne Patterson House, 522 Caroline Street; and the Bott House, 529 Caroline Street.

These houses show how a style, originating in nineteenth-century England as a revival of earlier forms, made its way to Key West, leaving a notable architectural legacy in our historic district.

The Bungalow

And now, an essay on the small, early twentieth-century house with a broad, sheltering roof and wide surrounding porches: the bungalow.

The form originated in India, where the Hindi word "bangla" refers to a house in the Bengal style. British colonial administrators noted the native form and had adaptations built as summer houses.

Meanwhile, in Britain, Victorian architecture reached its most ornate, exuberant and florid phase. A growing vanguard of people were weary of the perceived decorative excesses and shoddy craftsmanship of the time, and by the 1890s a stylistic rebellion was setting in—the Arts and Crafts movement—calling for a renewed simplicity and honesty in design and execution.

Into this mix, the tropical bungalow entered the mainstream of western architecture. British designers infused the form with traditional northern European features: stone fireplaces, dark paneling and hammered copper hardware.

By the early twentieth century, Americans were adopting bungalows as their own. California perfected the form, especially under the influence of the Greene brothers, architects who designed and built beautiful homes in Pasadena displaying meticulous artisanship.

A wider audience learned about bungalows through such publications as *The Craftsman* by Gustav Stickley, who included plans. Kit bungalows, including pre-cut lumber, were also available from large mail order companies, such as Sears, Roebuck and Montgomery Ward. A 1908 model, for example, cost $999. Soon homeowners were building bungalows from coast to coast.

Bungalows remained popular through the First World War. As the 1920s advanced, though, their popularity faltered, while in the thirties the Great Depression and changing tastes brought the bungalow era to a close.

Bungalows take on several different forms. Some have a gable roof, with the ridgeline running parallel to the street, with a low, sweeping roof covering a deep front porch. In these cases, a wide dormer often faces the street with a gable, hip or shed roof. Examples in Key West are 1021 Fleming Street, 922 Eaton Street and 809 to 817 Whitehead Street. Other bungalows have a front-facing gable with the ridge running perpendicular to the street. Sometimes in this instance the porch may project forward under a smaller, slightly off-center gable roof. This style can be found at 710 White Street or 632 William Street. Still other bungalows have a low-pitch hip roof, such as 910 Georgia Street.

Bungalows are generally small in scale, of only one or one-and-a-half stories. This type of house enjoyed wide popularity among middle-class homeowners, and their size reflects this demographic. Even those that are larger (like 415 Margaret Street) present a low, modest face to the street. In addition, bungalows invariably have one or more porches—reflective of their tropical origins—typically with massive tapering columns, square in profile, frequently set on high piers. Some bungalows also feature decorative pergolas or trellises, such as at 700 White Street.

Another notable feature is at the eave line where the roof meets the wall: the rafters are typically exposed rather than boxed in. In addition, on gable ends, some feature decorative, faux-functional brackets, seemingly "supporting" the overhanging roof. These elements reflect an interest in the visual elements of framing and structure. Moreover, windows may be double-hung with the upper sash divided into a number of panes (usually three), while the lower sash contains just one pane.

Finally, bungalow interiors feature an open plan, sometimes with rooms joined by wide rectangular arches flanked by square, tapered columns, similar to those on the front porch. Dark wood paneling or sheathing and even fireplaces are also typical of the style.

The City of Key West lists fifty-three bungalows in its inventory of historic buildings. Other examples stand on Pigeon Key and on the ocean side of Tavernier.

For further information, see *American Bungalow* magazine and its website (www.americanbungalowmagazine.com), which also sells related books.

The American Foursquare

Nearly a hundred years ago, a new form of house became popular, examples of which can be found in the Keys: the American Foursquare, or simply the Box.

Picture a two-story, wood-frame house, virtually cubic in form, surmounted by a pyramid (hip) roof with deeply overhanging eaves. Add a front porch—one-story for single-family houses, two-story for multi-unit structures. Frequently, porch posts are massive, tapered, square columns rising from high masonry bases. In the attic, a hip-roofed dormer is sometimes found. These are the basic ingredients of a classic American Foursquare.

The origins of this form of house lie in a rebellion against late Victorian architecture, when American houses displayed an unprecedented decorative exuberance. Designers cannibalized different architectural styles to create some of the most eclectic structures ever created.

By the turn of the last century, pioneering early modern architects like Frank Lloyd Wright (1869–1959) broke with the past, designing markedly simpler forms, pointing the way toward a sparer, distinctly twentieth-century idiom. The resulting Prairie style took its cues not from the pages of European architectural history but from the vast American landscape—a new architecture for a new continent.

Early examples of the style emerged initially in the Midwest, though it spread rapidly through pattern books, popular magazines and mail order companies selling complete kit houses.

Books and magazines influenced taste by publishing the new form to an audience of potential builders and homeowners, typically including floor plans and elevations.

Meanwhile, big Midwestern mail order companies, such as Sears, Roebuck, and Company in Chicago, offered whole houses for sale in kit form at reasonable prices. Pre-cut lumber, windows, doors, stairs, moldings and all the trimmings for a complete home sold as a convenient package for assembly by local contractors in small towns across America.

In Key West, the City's inventory of historic buildings lists twenty-eight Box-style homes, including the Curry Mansion Annex at 512 Caroline Street, Alexander's Guest House at 1118 Fleming Street and the Lofton Sands African Bahamian Museum and Resource Center at 324 Truman Avenue. Other examples can be found at 1125 Flagler Avenue and at 617 Angela, 829 Eaton, 328 Elizabeth, 504 Grinnell, 1209 Petronia, 707 Simonton, 811 Southard and 540 White Streets. There is also an American Foursquare on Conch Key. At least one example in Key West is said to be a Sears house.

These structures date from around 1905 to the Second World War. Because of its simplicity, this form of house proved very economical to build and remained popular through the Depression.

Today, it is still a handsome, practical form of house with the added luster of being historic.

Mediterranean Revival Style

One of the most important styles on the mainland of South Florida during the 1920s was the Mediterranean Revival style, which left a modest but discernable impact in the Keys.

The style emerged in the Southern United States, flourishing in a decade of unprecedented prosperity and mobility when Americans had more disposable income and more widely available means of transportation than ever before.

Much of this new travel occurred from North to South, a trend that especially benefited Florida, where rapid new development gave birth to an economic boom with colossal impacts even by the standards of the already bullish 1920s. Railroads carried visitors from one end of the state to the other and along both coasts, with Henry M. Flagler's line running from Jacksonville to Key West and Henry B. Plant's system serving the Gulf Coast.

Since tourists required accommodation as well as transportation, the major rail companies erected impressive hotels along their routes, thereby buttressing two mutually beneficial enterprises. St. Augustine, Tampa, Palm Beach and Key West all saw lavish resorts rising to cater to a well-heeled clientele. Meanwhile, Northerners seeking a more permanent base in Florida bought homes in the new communities of Coral Gables, Hollywood and Venice.

In this context, constructing buildings in a Mediterranean style made sense as developers promoted South Florida as "America's Riviera," employing an architectural vocabulary to suggest—and recreate—the established, posh resorts on the sun-drenched coasts of Spain, France and Italy. The style also traded on Florida's Spanish colonial heritage and maximized parallels between the climates of southern Europe, Latin America and Florida. Red-tiled roofs, stuccoed walls, casement windows, earth colors, wrought-iron hardware and massive wooden doors stand out as the hallmarks of this style.

Key West followed the spirit of the time, especially when the Overseas Railroad opened in 1912. The Florida East Coast Hotel Company envisioned a grand, first-class resort at the southern terminus of the Key West Extension, hiring the noted New York architectural firm of Carrere and Hastings to prepare the design. Given a Spanish name, the Casa Marina rose as the best example of the Mediterranean Revival in Key West, opening on New Year's Eve 1920. Then as now, the exterior features ochre-colored stucco walls, red-tile roofing and lush tropical landscaping, while the interior boasts a lobby, ballroom and dining room finished with dark wood paneling, beamed and coffered ceilings and massive stone fireplaces.

Hotel La Concha, also with a Spanish name, opened in 1926 with a less elaborate design. Nevertheless, it still displayed the signature decorative red tiles and stucco walls of the Mediterranean Revival.

Some Key West builders erected houses in this mode, too. A particularly fine example stands on Southard Street near Grinnell Street across from the Five Brothers Grocery. Additionally, a discrete row on the upper reaches of Von Phister Street nestles behind garden walls, while a group of homes on Eagle Avenue is as fine as any in the historic district.

These examples soon stood out as distinctive creations of their time as historical events swept onward, leaving the palmy days of the twenties behind. The 1926 hurricane dealt the first fatal blow to the boom in south Florida. Even though this storm did not hit Key West directly, the economic shockwaves it caused reverberated across the region.

By 1929 the stock market crash devastated financial prospects nationwide, putting an end to the Roaring Twenties and the Mediterranean Revival style. By the time prosperity returned, architectural ideas had changed, with subsequent development utilizing the more up-to-date Art Deco, Art Moderne and International styles.

For additional information on this and other architectural styles, see *A Field Guide to American Houses* by Virginia and Lee McAlester and *House Styles in America* by James C. Massy and Shirley Maxwell.

The Bahamian Connection

"Conch," as I need remind no one, signifies a native of the Florida Keys. Yet Bahamians also call themselves conchs, and this dual meaning suggests a close linkage between these two island groups.

Indeed, the Bahamas are one of the cultural hearths, or sources, of the Keys. Their history is the first chapter of our own, and our economy, architecture and population are, to a remarkable extent, very much related to our neighbors across the Gulf Stream.

As low-lying coral islands, prone to hurricanes and surrounded by extensive shallows and reefs, the Bahamas possess a natural history, geology and climate similar to the Keys.

Although the Spanish claimed the Bahamas, they made no concerted effort to settle the archipelago. Instead, the English moved in. Eleuthera was the first area of settlement, seeing the arrival in 1648 of Puritans who founded the communities of Governor's Harbour and Harbour Island. Spanish Wells also sprung up nearby in the late seventeenth century. Farther afield, what we now know as Nassau was founded in the late 1660s.

The Bahamas remained a remote outpost of British civilization for the next century.

The American Revolution (1775–1783), however, brought great changes, as American colonists loyal to vanquished Britain looked for a new home. With a warm climate and the possibility of a plantation economy, the Bahamas proved a popular destination for these refugees and their slaves, particularly from the Southern states, resulting in a remarkable increase in the Bahamian population.

These new arrivals in the 1780s crowded into existing settlements in Eleuthera; founded new towns in Abaco such as Hope Town on Elbow

Cay and New Plymouth on Green Turtle Cay; and established and worked on cotton plantations in the southern Bahamas.

The economy of the region had several aspects: agriculture provided essential fruits and vegetables as well as cash crops such as cotton, tobacco and sisal (a fiber for making rope). In addition, fishermen harvested turtles, conch, sponges, crawfish and other species from the sea, while industrious craftsmen developed shipbuilding, particularly in Abaco. Moreover, wrecking brought in goods that could be used locally or sold abroad.

Traditional buildings in the Bahamas evolved as small, simple and well-proportioned structures of wood construction inside and out. They featured clapboard siding, wood shingle roofs, sash windows, shady porches, narrow dormers and both side- and top-hinged shutters.

The nineteenth century brought new changes and challenges. Beginning in 1816, a series of lighthouses rose in the Bahamas, resulting in fewer wrecks. By 1825, the U.S. Congress passed a law specifically aimed at stemming the outflow of American wealth to the Bahamas and Cuba, requiring wreckers to bring any American ship wrecked on the Florida reef into an American port for salvage. Moreover, the British abolished slavery in 1834, effectively putting an end to plantation-dependent enterprises.

Meanwhile, Florida became an American territory in 1819, and many Bahamian wreckers joined the fledgling settlements taking hold on Key West and Indian Key beginning in the 1820s. Some of these early settlers included those with family names now common in the Keys: Albury, Bethel, Russell, Pinder and Sawyer.

Bahamian buildings in Key West particularly reflect the efforts of settlers from Green Turtle Cay. Most notably, two brothers-in-law from that island reputedly moved their houses here in 1847: the John Bartlum House at 730 Eaton Street and the Richard Roberts House at 408 William Street.

Other natives of Green Turtle Cay built their dwellings here, employing the style of their homeland, as seen in John Curry's snug cottage from the 1840s at 311 William Street, William and Eliza Saunders's ample home from the 1850s at 709 Eaton Street and Richard Moore Kemp's 1880s manse at 601 Caroline Street.

Meanwhile, John Lowe Jr. (whose father was born on Green Turtle Cay) erected a dignified residence at 620 Southard Street. And the Peacon family, also with Bahamian antecedents, built houses at 320 Peacon Lane and 712 Eaton Street.

These buildings testify to the Bahamian legacy in Key West, an inheritance from common conch ancestors. We who follow are fortunate to enjoy this island heritage.

Key West and New England

Looking at the well-proportioned clapboard houses painted white with green shutters, many observers correctly conclude that Key West has some sort of historical link to New England. Numerically, the most significant groups of settlers to Key West were Bahamians and Cubans. Yet there was a noteworthy minority of New Englanders too, and due to their maritime interests, early arrival and relative wealth, they played an important role in the community.

This is not surprising, since New England had a long tradition of fishing, shipbuilding and trade, and New Englanders sailed to many faraway ports to pursue their sea-related enterprises.

During the 1820s, for instance, some two dozen fishing vessels from Connecticut plied Key West waters, including those skippered by Benjamin and James Sawyer; Austin and George Packer; and William Kemp.

Among the Sawyers, two from Mystic, Connecticut—James Sawyer (d. 1829) and Captain John H. Sawyer (d. 1843)—have gravestones in the cemetery.

The Packers lay nearby. Josephus F. Packer—also from Mystic, Connecticut—owned property near Front and Duval Streets, which he rebuilt following the 1859 fire. During the Civil War, he joined the Union Volunteer Corps, a military unit loyal to the North. The name of Packer Street preserves the memory of this family.

Best known as one of the early proprietors of Key West, Pardon Greene was descended from a noted Rhode Island family. His son William C. Greene is buried in the cemetery, while Greene Street pays homage to the family as a whole.

Mallory is probably the best-known family name with a New England connection. Charles John Mallory, a construction engineer from Mystic,

Connecticut, arrived in Key West in 1823 with his wife Ellen (1792–1855) and their son Stephen. Ellen ran an early boardinghouse that first stood on the north side of Fitzpatrick Street, then later on the south side of Duval Street, near Front Street. She is buried in the cemetery.

Stephen R. Mallory (1812–1873) grew up to become a U.S. senator (1850–1861) representing Florida. A clipper ship was also named for him, built in Key West and launched in 1856. During the Civil War, Mallory sided with the South, becoming secretary of the Confederate navy. In 1873, Mallory and Company inaugurated steamship service to Key West. Mallory Square keeps this family name alive in Key West.

The Tifts were another prominent family of Connecticut Yankees. Amos C. Tift built a ships' chandlery, which survives as the oldest commercial building in town, now housing the Key West Chamber of Commerce. Later, Charles and Asa Tift operated an icehouse next door that held natural ice shipped from Maine. Like Stephen Mallory, Asa Tift supported the Southern cause during the Civil War, leaving Union-occupied Key West for the duration. Eventually, he returned to build the house with unusual masonry on Whitehead Street that Ernest Hemingway would later own.

The early history of the Baptist Church, which first gathered in 1842, is an institutional example of a connection to New England. As no other church of this denomination existed in Florida at this time, it affiliated with the Second Baptist Church of North Stonington, Connecticut. This relationship ended when the moral question of slavery divided the denomination before the Civil War.

It is interesting to observe how the Civil War presented a choice to the sons of New England in Key West. Some identified with the South and supported the Confederate cause, even if they still had cousins up north on the other side. Others cleaved to their original cultural and political heritage, remaining loyal to the Union.

Shortly after the Civil War ended, Peter Williams (1838–1899), a carpenter from New Bedford, Massachusetts, built what is now known as the Donkey Milk House on Eaton Street. Williams later served as a federal marshal in 1889. Following his death ten years later, he was laid to rest in the cemetery.

Another family with a connection to New Bedford were the Mitchells, who arrived in the early twentieth century. John Wallace Mitchell (1885–1929) came to the Keys to help build the Overseas Railway. He and other family members are interred in an impressive brick vault in the cemetery.

In reviewing this heritage, we can see how New Englanders contributed to the rich tapestry of Key West over the course of its history.

Key West and the South

Many different groups settled Key West, influencing local culture, politics and architecture in a variety of ways. Bahamians, New Englanders and Cubans each made their own contribution to the history of the Island City. Additionally, a number of Southerners made an imprint on Key West and left a lasting legacy.

Sandy Cornish (1793–1869) was born in Maryland as a slave. In 1839 he was moved to Florida, where his wife Lilah helped him buy his freedom. He experienced a major setback when a fire destroyed his free papers during the 1840s. When six men threatened to sell him back into slavery, he took a defiant stand in the public square of Port Leon. He mutilated himself—to render himself useless as a slave—by cutting off the fingers on his left hand, severing the muscles in his ankle and stabbing his hip. Friends nursed him back to health. He and his wife settled as free people in Key West during the late 1840s. Soon they acquired some land in an undeveloped area near what is now Truman Avenue, planting an orchard that flourished. He also helped found a church that would later be named in his honor: The Cornish Memorial AME Zion Church at 702 Whitehead Street.

Walter C. Maloney (1813–1884) grew up on a plantation in Georgia, although he was of Irish parentage. As he came to maturity, he realized that he did not want to exploit slaves to make his living. He left Georgia, settled in Key West and became a lawyer. Throughout his life, he retained his anti-slavery position. During the Civil War, he supported the Union, organizing a militia unit of men who were loyal to the North. Paradoxically, one of his sons fought for the Confederacy, and father and son were estranged for a while. In 1876 Maloney wrote the first history of Key West. He and his wife Mary are buried in the Key West Cemetery. Their house still stands at 725 Truman Avenue, on the grounds of the Key Lime Inn.

Joseph Beverly Browne (1814–1888) was born in Virginia. He graduated from the College of William and Mary at the age of sixteen and immediately moved to Key West. Soon he became involved in a host of local and territorial affairs, serving as a delegate to the St. Joseph's convention, a gathering that drafted what would eventually become the first constitution for the new State of Florida. In 1840 he married Mary Nieves Ximinez of St. Augustine. During the Civil War, he was a staunch partisan of the South. Afterward, he entertained the former president of the Confederacy at his home in Key West. Browne and his wife are buried in the Key West Cemetery. Their house no longer stands, a casualty of the 1886 fire.

Jeptha Vining Harris (1839–1914) was born in South Carolina and grew up in North Carolina and Mississippi. After college and medical school, he served as a surgeon in the Confederate army and navy. Later, he settled in Key West where he served as the collector of customs, both working and living at the first Custom House, which now stands at 124 Duval Street. After a while, he renewed his medical practice, living and working at 217 Duval Street, a building currently housing Cheeseburger Key West. Harris also worked to improve the early public school system and served as its superintendent. Harris School, built in 1909 on Southard Street, was named for him. He is buried in the Key West Cemetery.

This sampling of people from the South hints at the diversity of perspectives they contributed. Many Southern whites supported the Confederacy during the Civil War—but not all. And many Southern blacks were slaves—but not all.

Architecture in Key West certainly bears the stamp of the South, probably for both cultural and climatic reasons. People naturally built in the pattern to which they were accustomed. But even those from other regions adopted traditions that were suitable for hot weather: porches, both upstairs and down, to provide plenty of outdoor living area; high ceilings to allow hot air to rise above the inhabitants below; and separate kitchen outbuildings to isolate the heat of cooking away from the main house.

In this way, we can appreciate the extent to which Key West is a Southern city, in addition to being the Southernmost City.

Key West, Cuba and Preservation

Key West's history is inextricably linked with that of Cuba, the result of political turmoil and economic enterprise that left behind a cultural and architectural legacy that still looms large here today.

Revolutionaries seeking freedom from an oppressive Spanish colonial government arrived here in large numbers during the last third of the nineteenth century, taking advantage of the close proximity of the two islands only ninety miles apart. Following the inexplicable explosion in Havana Harbor of the USS *Maine*—some of whose dead lie at the Key West cemetery—the U.S. joined the struggle against Spain, helping tip the balance toward Cuban independence in 1898.

The Cuban presence in Key West added a new layer to the cultural strata of the community. What had been an English-speaking Protestant settlement with mostly Bahamian forebears experienced an infusion of Spanish-speaking Roman Catholic families with Cuban antecedents.

Cuban immigration also coincided with profound economic changes in Key West. The wrecking industry that had initially brought wealth here was in decline, as lighthouses, accurate charts and steam-powered ships led to a reduced need for salvaging. Meanwhile, new industrial capitalists combined with a Cuban labor force and Cuban tobacco to lay the seeds of the cigar-making industry, opening a new chapter in the economic history of the Island City.

Indeed, the legacy of the cigar-making business casts a long shadow here, as the remaining examples of these enterprises demonstrate.

The cigar factories themselves are, of course, a key element in this story. Three remaining examples of this building type are particularly notable. At the corner of Catherine and Grinnell Streets, a three-story brick factory provided different levels for drying tobacco, making cigars and packing and storing the finished product. At the corner of Staples Avenue and Second Street, the Martinez Havana Company constructed a two-story concrete facility with roughcast walls that resemble stone. And at the corner of Simonton and Virginia Streets, Eduardo Gato replaced an earlier wooden building destroyed by fire with a large, two-story poured concrete structure built around a courtyard that currently serves as county offices.

Worker housing is yet another significant category of buildings associated with cigar making and Cubans. Companies built small, one-story cigar makers' cottages to lease or sell to employees on favorable terms. Almost invariably narrow buildings with a linear plan, they feature a front porch facing the street and a series of rooms extending deeply into the lot. Most are of wood and covered with gable roofs, although some concrete block, hip-roofed examples also exist. Houses typically stand in groups within walking distance of the cigar factories.

The mansions built for the captains of this new industry compose the third major architectural reminder of early Cuban enterprise in cigar making. The Francisco Marrero House at 410 Fleming Street, the Alfonso/Diaz Carrasco House at 1001 Eaton Street and the Gato House at 1209 Virginia Street all attest to the wealth that financed these elaborate late-Victorian residences.

Other reminders of Cuban history in Key West still stand, too. Cuban cigar manufacturers capitalized First National Bank (now Wachovia) at the corner of Duval and Front Street in 1891, building in an ornate Moorish Revival style. Cuban Catholics contributed mightily to the growth of St. Mary Star of the Sea Church. And Cuban social and cultural organizations constructed distinctive headquarters such as the San Carlos Institute and the Cuban Club.

Cuban history is written in the cityscape just as it is in books. Understanding this story helps us appreciate the authentic links to the past that endure now and into the future.

Black History and Historic Preservation

Let's take a look at the past achievements, present status and future viability of black communities in the Keys and examine their significance in the context of historic preservation.

Considering these issues leads to a reexamination of the principles and strategies of historic preservation. Indeed, an understanding of the multi-racial character of the Keys goes right to the heart of basic questions in this field: Preservation of what? By what means? In what manner? For whom? And to what end?

Blacks arrived in the Keys at the beginning of settlement in the 1820s. Most came as slaves, their freedom delayed until emancipation in the 1860s. Jim Crow laws, segregation and even lynching followed.

Despite these difficulties, resilient black communities endured and flourished throughout the Keys. Bahama Village in Key West, Adderley Town in Marathon and many other smaller communities thrived.

In Key West, black Bahamians formed a community dotted with houses, workshops, service industries, churches, schools and fraternal organizations. Eventually, a black middle class emerged, leaving behind the legacy of slavery, achieving success in a variety of professions and trades and coming to own property.

In Marathon, George Adderley settled in a hardwood hammock on Crane Point on the bay side, building a house that still stands. Around him, a small village sprung up bearing his name. On nearby Pigeon Key, the presence of the "Negro" workers' quarters testifies to the fact that some of the labor force required to build the Overseas Railroad was black.

The current status of these communities varies. Many blacks left Monroe County, seeking greater opportunity or cheaper housing elsewhere. A long time ago, Adderley Village disappeared, with only its founder's house preserved as a museum. Today, Bahama Village exists as a living community, retaining a remarkable degree of historic integrity, though change seems inevitable.

A robust economy combined with easy mobility have fueled a demand for real estate, propelling values to previously unimagined heights. Faced with this boom—and such a limited supply of properties—Bahama Village is clearly experiencing the impact of these forces.

In the past, before urban neighborhoods experienced revitalization and restoration, landowners and developers bought out or evicted minority populations, often forcing them into public housing projects elsewhere. When this process of gentrification runs its course, the buildings remain but the earlier community ceases to exist.

Alternatively, both buildings and people may continue together, if the economic foundation of both is secure. A workable solution requires acknowledging and taking into account economic realities. Any means of softening the impacts of sharply appreciated (and unaffordable) property values must be practical. Moreover, the economic success of neighborhood residents is essential.

Several local initiatives attempt to address these problems. The Bahama Conch Community Land Trust owns housing units that it offers at an affordable rate, while others are being developed. This formula works since the nonprofit organization owns the underlying land, removing it from the speculative real estate market. A land trust rents or sells the housing units on it for the express purpose of providing affordable housing.

Economic development allowing previously disadvantaged people to participate in the larger economy is a greater challenge. A rising tide floats all boats; yet some people clearly see far greater benefit than others.

Community leaders are tackling this question in a variety of ways. The Land Trust has received grant moneys to teach marketable skills in the community. Moreover, property owners, business leaders and politicians are working to include Bahama Village in the tourist-driven economy.

Hopefully, through these efforts and others, involving people from all walks of life, true preservation that includes both historic buildings and traditional communities will continue into the future.

The Legacy of the Jewish Community

The origins of the Jewish community in Key West stem from anti-Semitic persecution in Eastern Europe, especially in Russia and Romania during the 1880s. Many refugees came to America, and some were attracted to Florida's largest and wealthiest city: Key West.

Like most immigrants, they started modestly, in this case working as peddlers. By 1891 the city enacted a whopping $1,000 license fee for all peddlers, which effectively drove them out of business. Responding to this, retail trade moved into shops and prospered.

During the early twentieth century, Jews in Key West bought a private house at the corner of Southard and Simonton Streets and adapted it for use as a synagogue. Additionally, a few years later community members founded a new secular organization: the Young Men's Hebrew Association.

By the end of the First World War, the Jewish community in Key West had coalesced and stabilized, as persecutions in Eastern Europe temporarily tapered off and immigration slowed. By this time, the first generation of families had established themselves and put down solid roots.

Among these are some familiar names: Wolfson, Appelrouth, Wolkowsky, Einhorn. Most were involved in the retail trade, especially dry goods.

The Jewish community prospered during the 1920s, reflecting larger economic trends. And along with the rest of the country, they struggled through the Depression during the following decade. Some families eventually moved north to Miami, as that city saw unprecedented growth. Gradually the center of gravity for the Jewish community in south Florida shifted toward the mainland.

World events accelerated this trend, with the rise of fascism in Europe resulting in large waves of Jewish immigrants to America, where they settled in larger cities.

Key West's well-established Jewish community hardly withered away, though. Congregation B'nai Zion built a new synagogue in the late 1960s. Additionally, the influx of newcomers to Key West during the last three decades injected new blood into the community. The arrival of Israelis brought about the founding of a new congregation.

Even families that moved away maintained their connections to Key West. Mr. and Mrs. Mitchell Wolfson painstakingly restored the Audubon House during the 1950s, a pioneering example of historic preservation at that time. A family foundation based in Miami continues to support this important museum.

Here are some landmarks in Key West's Jewish history to look for:

The Jewish section of the Key West cemetery features graves dating to the 1890s. Here are distinctive burial traditions: the placement of stones on the graves, Hebraic epitaphs and stars of David and menorahs carved onto the stones. Additionally, there is no cremation or aboveground interment.

The old synagogue at 530 Simonton Street at the corner of Southard served as a community center and sacred place. The original assembly hall is clearly visible on Southard Street, where Tudor arches crown the large windows, hinting at the Gothic Revival style. The building was used for services until 1969, when the congregation moved into a new synagogue on United Street. The old structure now houses Sarabeth's restaurant.

In addition to these important public landmarks, a number of local homes and shops have connections to Jewish history. At 729 Whitehead Street, a simple frame vernacular house dating from around 1874 served as the home and shop for Isaac Schvartz, listed in the 1893 city directory as a dealer in soda water. It is now part of the Historic Hideaways complex. Nearby, at 706 Duval Street a commercial building constructed circa 1906 served as the dry goods store of Gutman Kirchik. Born in 1875, he came from Romania to Key West in 1890, initially working at a shop with his brother. This building now houses Capricorn Jewelry and a designer shoe store.

A block away at 600 Duval Street stands another store dating from around 1906, where Frank Hotzberg ran his business. He also came from Romania, beginning life here as a peddler. The building, still used as a shop, displays a mezuzah on the doorpost, a small scroll with Biblical inscriptions, indicating continued use by a Jewish owner.

At 526–528 Duval Street, at the corner of Appelrouth Lane, the Lewinsky family built a masonry vernacular commercial building during the early 1920s. It still houses shops, also featuring a mezuzah in the doorway.

Many other shops and houses associated with the Jewish community members in Key West no longer stand: Aronovitz's dry goods, Appel's clothing store, Markovitz's grocery, Wolfson's Store of Fashion, Mulberg's bar. Yet the contribution of the Jewish community to Key West is unmistakable, and with a little looking observers today can still see tangible remains of this history.

Historic Preservation and the Gay Community

And now we turn to consider the impact that the gay community has had on the preservation and revitalization of Key West.

Christopher Cox wrote in *The Key West Companion*, "In the late seventies, a member of the Historic Preservation [*sic*] estimated that 70 percent of the restoration and renovation in Key West was being done by gay people…" While this statement is almost certainly impossible to verify, it is a provocative jumping off point for discussion.

The 1950s were an unfriendly time for both gays and preservationists. In Key West, the navy base formed the basis of economic life. At the same time, Tennessee Williams—one of the most adventurously gay writers of the decade—bought a small, historic cottage on Bahama Street and had it moved up to Duncan Street. His exploits here are now the stuff of legend.

During the 1960s, the era of youth culture and rebellion laid the foundation for the modern gay movement. Here, the social demographics began to change, as old-timers noticed the impact of the new philosophy: turn on, tune in and drop out.

By the 1970s, the gay movement was flourishing and gays came to Key West in large numbers. Hanns Ebensten, a pioneer in gay travel then living in New York, founded a company in 1972 that brought gay visitors to Key West. He moved here in 1978, acquiring a small historic house. Meanwhile, Key West was in a state of transition, as the navy closed many of its facilities, Old Town was officially designated a historic district and business leaders began looking toward tourism. Owners of businesses with a gay clientele, such as Walt Marlowe, founded the Key West Business Guild in 1978 to promote gay tourism.

During the 1980s, gays consolidated many of their gains, benefiting from an increasing sense of community and economic power. Locally, Richard Heyman's election as mayor symbolized this progress. At the same time, this was also the first decade of AIDS, and many were lost, including Heyman.

By 1984, the "Gayellow Pages," a gay travel directory, listed a number of businesses—mostly guesthouses—in historic buildings:

The Banyan, 323 Whitehead Street, took over the old Delaney house, a Queen Anne style manse that is now a time-share.

The Curry House, 806 Fleming Street, was established in a frame house long occupied by a branch of that Key West family.

The Cypress House, 601 Caroline Street, took its name from its beautiful unpainted wood siding. Richard Moore Kemp had the house built after an earlier structure burned in the 1886 fire.

The Gideon Lowe House, 409 William Street, bore the name of an early occupant of that circa 1866 house.

La Terraza De Marti, 1125 Duval Street, was the nickname for the Teodoro Perez house, where Cuban revolutionary Jose Marti once spoke from the balcony.

Then as now, the Oasis of Key West, 823 Fleming Street, occupied a handsome circa 1874 historic house.

The Palms of Key West, 820 White Street, operated out of a circa 1889 Queen Anne style building.

The Victorian House, 410 B Fleming Street, took its name from the heyday of Key West architecture.

There was also a popular gay bar in a historic building: the Copa, 623 Duval Street, in the old Monroe Theater. Regrettably, this landmark burned down ten years ago.

Other historic buildings, too, benefited from gay endeavors. The former Kress five-and-dime on Duval Street gained a new lease on life as Fast Buck Freddie's. And a frame building at 1215 Petronia Street became the home of the Metropolitan Community Church.

Private homes, too, saw increasing rehabilitation by gays, who joined preservation organizations, served on the Historic Architectural Review Commission and won preservation awards.

The Richard Roberts house at 408 William Street—said to have been moved here from the Bahamas—served as the home of Berry Tracy, a curator at the Metropolitan Museum, and his partner.

A pair of matching houses at 701 and 703 Fleming Street saw rehabbing by Jerry Herman, the famous composer and lyricist of Broadway musicals, and his partner.

Ferdinand Coudert, a noted international lawyer and linguist, and his partner thoroughly renovated the magnificent W. Hunt Harris House at 425 Caroline Street.

The landmark "Octagon" house at 712 Eaton Street—long the home of the Peacon family—experienced a lavish redo under the care of Angelo Donghia, an interior designer who sold it to fashion designer Calvin Klein.

In reviewing these examples, one can begin to appreciate the impact that the gay community has had on the preservation of Key West.

On the topic generally, see *A Passion to Preserve: Gay Men as Keepers of Culture* by Will Fellows. For a history of a gay resort community, see *Cherry Grove, Fire Island: Sixty Years in America's First Gay and Lesbian Town* by Esther Newton. For Key West, see the oral history video tapes and scrapbooks at the Gay and Lesbian Community Center.

Preserving Historic Lighthouses

Out of site, out of mind. That attitude, some preservationists say, has placed the Florida Keys historic reef lighthouses in the condition that they are in today: neglected and forgotten. How many of us realize that some of the most significant engineering projects of the nineteenth century took place in the Florida Keys?

In order to curb the legendary wrecks on the Florida Reef—misfortunes that made Key West rich while also taking a terrible toll on shipping—the United States government embarked on an ambitious and experimental program. Army engineers designed and built lighthouses directly on the reef itself, even if there was little or no land above water on which to place the foundations.

George Gordon Meade, a young army officer who would later lead Union troops to victory at the Battle of Gettysburg during the Civil War, oversaw the first phase of the project in the 1850s, employing pioneering technology. Workers sunk iron screw piles into the bottom of the sea, creating a rigid open framework supporting the lighthouse keeper's quarters and the lantern with the light above. The lighthouses on Sand Key, Carysfort Reef and Sombrero Key were the first fruits of this construction program.

The Civil War temporarily interrupted the project in the 1860s. An additional phase of work resumed in the 1870s and '80s, resulting in the building of additional towers at Alligator Reef, Fowey Rocks, American Shoal and Rebecca Shoal.

Today, these historic engineering marvels still stand on the reef, warning mariners from the treacherous shallows nearby.

Other lighthouses were built, too. Cape Florida on Key Biscayne stands at the northeastern end of this chain, while Garden Key Light and

Loggerhead Key Light cluster at the extreme southwestern tip, in the Dry Tortugas. Additionally, Key West Light occupies a site at the heart of our historic district. Yet these latter structures are all on solid land and most of them are currently preserved as museums and open to the public.

The reef lights, however, stand far offshore, untended, isolated and vulnerable. To discourage vandalism at Rebecca Shoal Light, the Coast Guard removed the vacant keeper's house in the 1950s. More recently, Sand Key Light experienced a serious fire, damaging the structure.

Enter the Florida Keys Reef Lights Foundation, an organization founded to raise awareness of the plight of these important structures. They have organized boat trips to some of these remote outposts. Additionally, they hope to establish a museum that tells their story and to make the towers themselves more accessible to the public. And they are working with the Coast Guard—the stewards of these lights—to encourage preservation.

For centuries, lighthouses have inspired feelings of romance, solitude and adventure. Now with this new initiative in the Florida Keys, people with these sentiments can join with others to advance the cause of these landmarks' preservation. Love Dean Winslow, author of *Lighthouses of the Florida Keys*, aptly called such advocates "the new keepers of the lights."

For more information, go to www.floridalighthouses.org.

Preserving Historic Forts

Although maintaining even the smallest historic conch house in the Keys can feel like a continuous uphill struggle, imagine taking care of enormous brick fortifications that feature massively thick walls, remote and exposed locations and formidable repair demands. Regardless of these difficulties, forts often possess national significance, and a number of agencies are working to preserve them for future generations.

The idea of building forts in the Keys gained traction in the 1820s following the American acquisition of Florida, since the narrow sea passage between Florida and Cuba served as a critical link between the densely settled eastern seaboard and the resource-rich Mississippi Valley. Some observers considered the Keys "the Gibraltar of the Gulf," playing the same strategic role as the British fortress at the entrance to the Mediterranean Sea.

In Key West, construction began in 1845 of a fort later named for President Zachary Taylor. Though it was not yet complete by the outbreak of the Civil War in 1861, Major Brannan, an army commander in Key West, marched his men in the middle of the night from the barracks (at what is now Peary Court) to occupy the structure. Consequently, the fort—and Key West—remained in Northern control throughout the war.

The army built two additional forts in Key West, known as martelloes. (A "martello" is a circular masonry fort or blockhouse, named for Cape Martella in Corsica.) Each features a central tower surrounded by a curtain wall. A narrow-gage railway joined West Martello to Fort Taylor to transport heavy ordnance.

Meanwhile, in the Dry Tortugas sixty-eight miles west of Key West, construction of Fort Jefferson commenced in 1846. It, too, was incomplete at the onset of the Civil War and remained in Union control, serving as a prisoner of war camp. Following the assassination of President Lincoln in 1865, Fort Jefferson held men charged as accomplices to that crime. Dr. Samuel Mudd, who treated John Wilkes Booth for a broken leg after Booth had shot the president, was captive at Fort Jefferson for four years. During a yellow fever epidemic at the Fort, he ministered to both prisoners and guards alike, earning a presidential pardon in 1869.

By the late nineteenth century, the invention of rifled cannon rendered the old brick forts obsolete. The army cut down Fort Taylor from its original height of three stories, and Fort Jefferson became a coaling station.

The twentieth century saw various agencies take over and preserve these forts. In 1935 President Roosevelt proclaimed Fort Jefferson a National Monument. Fifteen years later, the Key West Art and Historical Society signed a lease with Monroe County for East Martello. Fort Taylor became a state park in 1976, with citizens soon forming the Friends of Fort Taylor to provide assistance. Additionally, the Key West Garden Club leased West Martello from the county.

Now these forts face a variety of preservation concerns.

Fort Taylor suffered from the removal of its upper levels, resulting in interior flooring becoming outdoor roofing. Incoming water gradually eroded mortar and rusted the heavy iron gun ports or embrasures, breaking apart the surrounding masonry. During the 1990s, workers rebuilt some of the parapets to prevent water damage and repointed one flank of this structure. Three other walls, however, still await repairs.

Fort Jefferson is suffering from similar deterioration. Moreover, as ironwork surrounding the cannon ports corrodes, special iron shutters fitted on either side of the openings are coming loose and plunging into the moat below. The fort's remote location as well as its great size—by some estimates, the largest brick structure in the Western Hemisphere—present additional obstacles. Responding to these problems, the National Park Service has prepared a detailed plan for significant repairs.

West Martello, located off Atlantic Boulevard, has suffered from its exposed location on Higgs Beach. Over the years, it has been stabilized and preserved in its existing condition with new steel supports under some of its arches. Additionally, the lack of proper rest room facilities plagued the facility for many years. A newly constructed red-brick structure now answers this need.

East Martello had long experienced water intrusion in its curtain wall, which, like Fort Taylor, was originally intended to have enclosed space above it. A later wooden roof covering gradually failed, only to receive further damage from Hurricane Georges in 1998. State grant funds helped pay for repairs, which included removing the wooden roof structure and resurfacing the curtain wall with lightweight concrete and a membrane. Such are the measures taken to protect this and other valuable historic forts for posterity.

Historic Navy Buildings

The recent transfer of the Truman Waterfront from the navy to the City of Key West provides an occasion to review the Southernmost City's naval history and architecture.

The navy has been a major player in Key West from the very beginning. Commodore David Porter, commander of the Anti-Pirate Squadron in 1822, selected a site near the waterfront and built a storehouse, workshop, hospital and barracks. These facilities were soon vacated, though, as Porter's rapid success in his mission combined with an outbreak of yellow fever led to the closing of the base in 1826. No buildings survive from this early period.

Additional health concerns prompted the construction in 1845 of the Marine Hospital (Quarters R), designed by architect Robert Mills. Nearly a century later, it experienced extensive alterations for conversion to multi-family housing. Recently redeveloped as condominiums, it is the oldest remaining building on the Naval Station.

By 1854 the navy had acquired more land, building a large brick depot on Front Street between 1856 and 1863. Serving as the Administration Building until 1932, it subsequently housed the Lighthouse Service and the Coast Guard before renovation as Clinton Square Market.

During the Civil War (1861–1865), the navy used Key West as a port for bringing in captured Confederate ships, undertaking few building projects.

Three decades later, the Spanish-American War (1898) coincided with a new spate of construction activity. One of the buildings from this era, the brick Machine Shop (Building 7), extends over two hundred feet along Front Street. Developers recently adapted it for use as town houses.

By 1902 the navy acquired the remaining land southwest of Whitehead Street between Fleming and Fitzpatrick Streets, constructing many new buildings, such as two brick structures on Front Street. Building 21, completed in 1902, saw use as an equipment storehouse, tool room, electrical workshop, sail and rigging loft and marine barracks. It now houses offices. Nearby, the navy erected Building 11 in 1904 as a smithery or foundry, which today does duty as a private home.

Meanwhile, on Whitehead Street the navy built handsome, wood-frame homes for officers: Quarters D (1904) and Quarters C (1906). Currently rehabilitated, they too serve as private homes.

A trio of concrete buildings also arose at this time. The Pump Plant of 1908, also known as Building 45, now functions as an office; Building 48, constructed in 1910 as a storehouse, has a new lease on life as the Mel Fisher Maritime Museum. The Weather Bureau (Quarters T) built in 1912 now welcomes guests as a hotel.

Following the American entry into World War I (1914–1918), Key West served as the headquarters for the Seventh Naval District, resulting in the construction of some more buildings.

Notable examples include three impressive two-story houses: Quarters M-1, a wood-frame structure on Whitehead Street from 1915; the Surgeon's Quarters (Quarters L), a masonry building on Front Street of 1918; and Quarters G, a wood-frame residence on Whitehead Street built in 1923. Currently rehabilitated, they now all serve as private homes.

With the coming of World War II (1941–1945), Key West experienced a huge influx of civilian and military war workers, fueling more construction.

The most impressive example from this era is the Administration Building (Building 124), a three-story, steel and concrete edifice erected in 1942, where nearly two decades later, President John Kennedy met with British Prime Minister Harold Macmillan. Now rehabilitated, the building houses condominiums.

In the late 1940s and early 1950s, President Harry Truman stayed at Quarters A, originally built in 1890 for the base commandant and paymaster. Truman made it his "Little White House" during a series of winter working vacations. Currently restored, it is open as a museum. This popularity with the president led officials to rename the Naval Station Truman Annex, a fitting designation for the core of the historic military base in Key West.

Preserving Historic Religious Buildings

For a town better known for vice than virtue, Key West sure does have a lot of churches. Yet given the importance of religion historically, it is not surprising. These landmark buildings stand in witness to the aspirations of our community in an earlier age. Today, they can pose difficult preservation challenges due to their high maintenance costs and the changing place of religion in modern society. It falls on us to devise creative and successful strategies for preserving these edifices for the future.

Settlers founded religious establishments soon after arriving here. Early Bahamian settlers formed large portions of the St. Paul's Episcopal, Methodist and Baptist Churches. The influx of Cubans following the outbreak of war in 1868 resulted in explosive growth for St. Mary Star of the Sea Catholic Church, the now defunct St. John's Episcopal Church and a Cuban Methodist Mission. At the same time, the growth of the black community following the Civil War saw the emergence of a number of African American churches, such as the Cornish Memorial AME Zion Church and St. Peter's Church. Meanwhile, a nascent Jewish community built a synagogue at the corner of Simonton and Southard Streets.

These buildings have been susceptible to damage from the beginning. The 1846 hurricane destroyed the first St. Paul's and Methodist churches. Fires erased the first Catholic church, the second St. Paul's and the Baptist church. Later hurricanes wiped out Sparks Chapel and the third St. Paul's.

Now preservation challenges of a different nature appear. Our increasingly secular and mobile society has left many of these congregations with diminishing attendance, dwindling financial support and massive deferred maintenance backlogs. Successful preservation strategies span a range from careful stewardship of existing resources to radical changes of use when the original use is no longer viable.

Perhaps the most radical change of use here was the conversion of the old Baptist church on Eaton Street to Club Chameleon, a nightclub where *Flamingo Follies*, an extravagant and irreverent costume revue, played for some time. Other conversions have less shock value. The old synagogue on Simonton Street currently houses Sarabeth's restaurant. The old Christian Science church on Truman Avenue does duty now as the Wesley House Community Center. A small stone Gothic Revival church on Whitehead Street shelters offices. And a little wooden church on Thomas Street serves as a capacious and distinctive home.

Some old buildings are preserved because new congregations move in to occupy different—but still historic—structures. The Christian Science Reading Room currently occupies a small, domestic-scale structure on Elizabeth Street. The Southernmost Prayer and Faith Center is now headquartered at the old Fleming Street Methodist Church. The Unitarian Universalist Fellowship currently meets in an old Cuban fraternal lodge building at the corner of Petronia and Georgia Streets. And the Metropolitan Community Church worships in a historic wooden building on Petronia Street.

Other churches in town continue to function in their historic headquarters, such as Old Stone, Trinity Presbyterian, St. Peter's and St. Mary's. Some have successfully sought out supplementary preservation funds from a variety of sources. St. Paul's Episcopal and the Southernmost Prayer and Faith Center obtained state grant moneys for structural and roof repairs. Meanwhile, the Cornish Memorial AME Zion Church found some repair funds available from the Old Island Restoration Foundation.

State preservation grant programs naturally are based on properties' historic and architectural significance, since government funding for churches' general operations would be unconstitutional. In Europe, where state religions own much of the ecclesiastical real estate, buildings are preserved as much for cultural as religious reasons. Whether here or abroad, people recognize that religious buildings have a significance beyond their sectarian histories, bearing witness to the faiths of earlier times while also offering a legacy that enriches contemporary communities.

Preserving Historic Schools

Old-time Key Westers know firsthand the importance of this topic, since the loss of one very historic school—Mary Immaculate on Truman Avenue—helped spark the current historic preservation movement here.

In 1878 the Catholic Church built an imposing edifice to house a parochial school and the nuns who taught there. During the Spanish-American War of 1898, the building served as a hospital for wounded soldiers. Over the years, generations of children from all religious backgrounds attended the institution, which stood in its distinctive quarters until 1968. Following its demolition, some Old Town homeowners salvaged sections of the porch balustrades to use as fences. Others saved the cupola on the roof, which now stands at ground level on the property.

Despite the loss of this landmark, we are still fortunate to have a number of historic schools remaining in our community. The oldest standing public school is Harris High School on Southard Street, built in 1909 and distinguished by its roughcast concrete walls resembling hewn blocks of stone. During the next decade, the school board built what was then called the Division Street Grammar School, more recently renamed the Harvey Government Center at the Historic Truman School. The 1920s saw two more schools constructed in Key West: the old Monroe County High School of 1923 (now Glynn Archer School) and the Reynolds Street School of 1927. In Bahama Village the recently renovated Frederick Douglass Band Room stands as a descendant of Key West's first black school, named for the great nineteenth-century abolitionist.

Besides the public schools, buildings that once housed private schools are also still standing, including the Baldwin house at the corner of Duval and Eaton Streets that is now the office of the Prudential Knight Keyside Properties. Farther down Duval Street in the area of town known as Gatoville, a small wooden structure once served as a schoolhouse in the 1890s. The San Carlos Institute, founded in the 1870s and offering some of the first racially integrated classes in Florida, moved into its current building in 1924.

Outside Key West, the school board built two sister schools following the 1935 hurricane. The Matecumbe School in Islamorada, currently the county library, and the Tavernier School, until recently the Health Department, stand out for their massive poured concrete walls enabling the bunker-like structures to serve as hurricane shelters.

Some of these buildings still serve as schools, while others have assumed new functions. Those structures fulfilling their original purpose are invariably at the center of students' lives; parents, too, inevitably become familiar with their hallowed halls. Reunion classes fortunate enough to still have an old school to return to marvel at being able to revisit old Miss So-And-So's classroom again, so replete with memories.

Schools often serve other purposes—polling places, hurricane shelters, concert halls—further reinforcing the significance of these buildings as centers of community life. Some see permanent adaptation to other uses, including government offices, libraries, businesses and clinics, attesting to the flexibility and creativity needed for developing new uses for these historic buildings.

The dual nature of schools' significance lies both in their intellectual mission and in their physical fabric. As schools, they are centers of education and the life of the mind. As historic buildings, they are architectural embodiments of a community's cultural history and values.

Preserving Historic Storefronts

Old commercial buildings are notable for being more visible and publicly accessible than private houses. Yet many of these significant structures have been subject to extensive alterations, especially their highly trafficked ground floors, entrances, display windows, signs and awnings. Modifications often followed changes in tenancy, architectural fashions and retailing trends.

Commercial architecture flourished during the nineteenth century, as advances in manufacturing—especially the development of plate glass—made possible large display windows. In Key West, stores are typically wood-frame structures abutting the sidewalk with shops downstairs, accessed by a recessed doorway topped by a transom and flanked by display windows. Low bulkheads stand between the sidewalk and the window, while a horizontal fascia overhead provides room for a sign. Upper floors may house residential units or storage, while the roof may not be visible, hidden by a high parapet or "boomtown" façade. The old sponge warehouse at the northern corner of Fleming and Margaret Streets is an example of this.

By the early twentieth century, concrete became popular, since it was resistant to fire, hurricanes, termites and rot. Examples of this new material include Bogart's, the Lewinsky Building and Fast Buck Freddie's, all on Duval Street.

Interiors sometimes boasted tin ceilings, tile floors and elaborate cabinetry and millwork.

Following the Second World War, this pattern changed as retailing shifted from a pedestrian and streetcar activity to one based on automobiles. Suburbanization brought about the development of shopping plazas and eventually fully enclosed malls with plenty of convenient parking. Many older commercial buildings declined or experienced radical alterations in attempts to lure customers otherwise inclined to seek newness and modernity.

In the last quarter-century, however, with the increased awareness of historic buildings and the revitalization of downtowns, many property owners have rehabilitated old commercial buildings capitalizing on their unique, attractive qualities.

A good first step in such a project is making an inventory of remaining historic features: windows, siding, doors, floors and ceilings. Much of what we know of buildings comes from evidence in the structures themselves. Clues may point toward historic uses and modifications.

Documentary research may also help. The library contains at least three sources: Sanborn fire insurance maps delineate the footprint of buildings and may include notes on use; historic photographs, if available, graphically represent the earlier appearance of structures; and city directories may indicate who operated the business and what they did. Even small tidbits of information from these sources may help in planning the rehabilitation.

Preparing a design that successfully integrates the building's historic character with the projected new use is both an art and a science. An architect with experience in historic preservation can be invaluable, especially if the building has seen extensive alterations or if large new additions are envisioned. Design professionals can also provide knowledge of the various codes while supplying important on-site supervision.

Construction itself often has two phases. Removing inappropriate alterations ("selective demolition") involves *subtraction*, such as getting rid of later aluminum cladding, huge interior-lit signs or dropped tile ceilings. This course of action may uncover more historic features, leading one to modify plans to preserve these discoveries.

Construction—the process of *addition*—comes next. Recreating lost historic elements may be in order if adequate photographic, documentary or physical evidence exists to guide the work. With no other signposts than conjecture, however, original new work is appropriate, provided it is both compatible with the historic features and differentiated from them.

Also important are the more transitory alterations and adaptations. Awnings providing shelter from sun and rain are traditional features of many old storefronts—as one can imagine in the days before air conditioning.

Signage, too, affects the historic character of historic commercial buildings, and if complementary in design and execution, it can enhance a project.

Sensitive consideration of the unique character of historic commercial buildings can ensure that they will grace our downtowns and earn their keep economically for many years to come.

Preserving Historic Industrial Buildings

Old factories and mills stand as relics of an earlier era, presenting singular preservation issues, as a variety of examples in Key West attest.

Large industrial buildings first rose in Key West in the middle of the nineteenth century, as the Industrial Revolution got under way. At that time, a new approach to manufacturing restructured society, placing formerly independent craftsmen and artisans within highly organized industrial operations.

The navy base saw some of the first industrial activities here, especially with the demise of wooden sailing ships and the rise of steel steamships, a technological change that required a substantial increase in infrastructure. The advent of cigar making further expanded the industrial base in Key West. Although not a heavy "smokestack" industry, cigar making took place on a large scale in a highly structured environment, resulting in the building of a number of big factories.

The decline of manufacturing and industry in Key West echoed similar trends across the country. Cigar making was dead by the Depression, while the navy closed much of the base in the 1970s. The economy changed, with an emphasis more on services, especially tourism, rather than manufacturing.

This economic shift left a legacy of large, vacant industrial buildings, presenting a host of challenging preservation projects.

One of the most daunting aspects of dealing with these structures is their size. With cavernous interiors, it may seem difficult to fill so much space.

Another obstacle to overcome is the traditionally low status of these buildings. Even before William Blake wrote of "dark, satanic mills," they occupied a place at the bottom of society's pecking order. Designers and patrons traditionally did not consider industrial buildings to exemplify real "architecture." Meanwhile, the preservation movement, emerging in part as a reaction against the Industrial Revolution, focused initially on saving pre-industrial sites. The movement largely ignored factories and industrial buildings, which remained until recently the poor cousins of preservation. These attitudes have made it difficult to see the potential that these buildings have.

Yet they have many advantages. The large expanses of uninterrupted interior space are usually free of elaborate architectural features that would otherwise interfere with a new function. Consequently, they present an essentially blank slate for adaptive use, readily lending themselves to a variety of novel purposes. Additionally, they are often massive "industrial strength" structures of masonry or concrete: noncombustible, termite proof and hurricane resistant.

Over the last several decades, Key West has seen some success stories in the preservation and reuse of many of its old industrial buildings.

Following the navy's withdrawal in 1974, a number of military structures on Front Street saw successful conversion to private civilian use. These examples of adaptive reuse are discussed above.

More recently, a relic of the cigar-making industry has benefited from a complete rehabilitation. The Gato cigar factory (which the navy extensively altered during and after World War II) saw a remarkable turnaround, as the County spearheaded a project to convert the vacant building to bustling government offices, restoring dozens of blocked up windows, opening up a central courtyard and sprucing up its grounds.

Other cigar factories—the Ferdinand Hirsh factory on Catherine Street and the Martinez-Havana factory on Staples Avenue—serve as moving and storage warehouses, still pulling their weight economically although having experienced some alterations.

Meanwhile, the façade of the old Steam Plant on Trumbo Road is being incorporated into luxury condominiums. Soon, it will join the ranks of workaday industrial sites that have a new and different lease on life.

Historic Movie Theaters

The invention of motion pictures brought about a new type of building: a theater for film, not for plays. Although initially following earlier forms, movie theaters soon developed their own style, reflecting the glamour of Hollywood. Especially during the Great Depression, fanciful façades boasting neon-lit marquees and ornate interiors featuring balconies and elaborate decoration heightened a sense of fantasy and escape.

In Key West, there were a number of movie theaters in Old Town:

The Strand, 527 Duval Street, is one of the most visible survivors. Originally built during the early 1920s, it initially exhibited a different façade than we see today. In 1926–27, a Spanish architect redesigned the lobby and the façade. Decorative masonry elements were cast in Cuba and shipped here, where Cuban laborers completed the work. A fire destroyed most of the interior in 1934, although the front was only slightly damaged. The neon "Strand" sign appeared in 1946. During the early 1990s, it housed the Ripley's Believe It Or Not Odditorium; more recently, Walgreens converted it to a drugstore.

In Bahama Village, the Lincoln Theater, 813 Emma Street, operated during segregation for a black audience. The simple façade reflected the "separate and unequal" economic and social status that its target clientele experienced. After desegregation, the establishment closed, and the building became a church. Currently, the structure serves as a studio for sculptor John Martini.

In 1924, the San Carlos Institute, 516 Duval Street, was not built specifically as a movie theater, but it had space for a variety of performances. And from the 1930s to early 1950s, it housed the Palace Theater with a neon marquee added to the older Baroque-Revival façade. Later, the building was restored to its earlier configuration. But even so, there was some continuity of use: the Key West Film Society showed films at this venerable venue until relatively recently.

The Monroe Theater, formerly at 623 Duval Street, was built sometime after 1912. It had a long career showing movies from the golden age of Hollywood. By the 1970s, however, it was reduced to showing X-rated films. It received a new lease on life—and served as a notable example of adaptive reuse—during the eighties, when it housed a popular nightclub, the Copa. Regrettably, it burned to the ground in a devastating fire in 1995. An art gallery now stands on the old site.

Meanwhile, in the Upper Keys, what is now the Tavernier Hotel, on the ocean side of U.S. 1 at mile marker 91.8, was originally conceived as a movie theater during the 1930s. Later it was converted to a lodging house. It is now one of the most visible buildings in the Tavernier Historic District.

With changing times, historic movie theaters face a number of challenging preservation issues, including scale, location and economic shifts. Nowadays, movies are typically screened in smaller spaces rather than the big movie palaces of yesteryear. Multiplexes are common, and parking is extremely important as locations in suburban shopping centers and malls surrounded by parking lots eclipse downtown sites. Finally, retail rents on busy commercial streets have sometimes climbed too high for uses that are essentially large rooms with no need for street frontage or shop windows.

For these reasons, the National Trust for Historic Preservation listed "Historic American Movie Theaters" on its 2001 list of America's Eleven Most Endangered Historic Places.

Yet many such buildings have managed to survive to the present day. Probably the best-preserved ones retain a function of housing large groups of people for performances of some kind. Adaptive reuse can help save other historic theaters, although care should be taken to make certain that the new use does not require drastic changes to the historic character of the building.

As we advance in the new millennium, appreciation for twentieth-century buildings is increasing. Hopefully, this trend bodes well for the long-term prospects for this unique type of architecture.

For more information, see *Cinema Treasures: A New Look at Classic Movie Theaters* by Ross Melnick and *The Southern Movie Palace: Rise, Fall, and Resurrection* by Janna Jones.

The Bahama House, 730 Eaton Street, is one of a handful of buildings said to have been moved to Key West from Green Turtle Cay in the Bahamas. The owner was a noted shipbuilder, John Bartlum. *Courtesy of the History Department, May Hill Russell Library, Key West.*

The Richard Roberts House, 408 William Street, is also believed to have been relocated to Key West from the Bahamas. During the 1980s, it belonged to Berry Tracy, a curator at the Metropolitan Museum in New York. *Courtesy of the History Department, May Hill Russell Library, Key West.*

John Geiger, a prosperous wrecker and harbor pilot, built this house at 205 Whitehead Street around 1850. It survived a nearby fire in 1859, when a neighbor blew up his own house to create a firebreak. The Mitchell Wolfson family restored the property during the 1950s. *Audubon House at 205 Whitehead Street. Courtesy of the History Department, May Hill Russell Library, Key West.*

The Ferguson House used to stand on Eaton Street. It is a good example of the Classical Revival style in Key West, with a gable front and a two-story porch with columns. In more recent times, it was moved to Truman Annex. *Courtesy of the History Department, May Hill Russell Library, Key West.*

William and Caroline Lowe, partisans of the South during the Civil War, built and lived in this house. Later, it served as an art gallery and as a restaurant. A fire in 1956 damaged the structure, which was subsequently demolished. *Courtesy of the History Department, May Hill Russell Library, Key West.*

The building of lighthouses in the Keys was a high priority for the federal government during the nineteenth century. This cast-iron tower marks Fort Jefferson in the Dry Tortugas, sixty-eight miles west of Key West. *Courtesy of the History Department, May Hill Russell Library, Key West.*

Military strategists considered the Keys "the Gibraltar of the Gulf," due to their strategic location at the entrance to the Gulf of Mexico. The presence of several forts, including Fort Jefferson, ensured that the Keys stayed in Union control during the Civil War. *Fort Jefferson. Courtesy of the History Department, May Hill Russell Library, Key West.*

Fort Jefferson features massive brick walls, a moat and a drawbridge. Some of the Lincoln conspirators—men accused of plotting to assassinate President Lincoln—were held here during the late 1860s. It is now a National Park. *Old Fort Jefferson on Dry Tortugas, near Key West. Courtesy of the History Department,*

The U.S. Army built the East Martello in Key West during the Civil War to ward off a Confederate attack. It features a central tower surrounded by a curtain wall. The property now houses an art and history museum. *Courtesy of the History Department, May Hill Russell Library, Key West.*

Asa Tift built this unusual stone house shortly after the Civil War. Tift was from New England but sided with the South during the war. During the 1930s, writer Ernest Hemingway lived and worked in this house, which is now open to the public. *907 Whitehead Street. Courtesy of the History Department, May Hill Russell Library, Key West.*

The Catholic Church built the Convent of Mary Immaculate during the 1870s to house nuns and a parochial school. During the Spanish-American War, it served as a hospital. In 1968 it was torn down, fueling a nascent historic preservation movement. *Front of Convent and driveway with arch. Courtesy of the History Department, May Hill Russell Library, Key West.*

A photograph from circa 1890 depicts a now vanished storefront at 101 Simonton Street in Key West. Nineteenth-century commercial buildings often featured recessed entrances, large display windows, hand-painted signs and roll-up awnings. *Courtesy of the History Department, May Hill Russell Library, Key West.*

Cigar making grew from a cottage industry to a major pillar of the economy during the later nineteenth century. Workers hand-rolled Cuban tobacco to make a product that undersold imported products. *Courtesy of the History Department, May Hill Russell Library, Key West.*

Cigar manufacturers often built rows of small cottages within walking distance of their factories to house workers. Although these houses may seem small by today's standards, cigar makers often raised large families in them. *Courtesy of the History Department, May Hill Russell Library, Key West.*

By the late nineteenth century, cigar manufacturers had built large factories, such as the Havana American factory shown here. Drying tobacco, rolling cigars and packing the finished product sometimes took place on the different floors of the building. *Courtesy of the History Department, May Hill Russell Library, Key West.*

Some cigar manufacturers such as Francisco Marrero profited handsomely from the business. Marrero built his house at 410 Fleming Street in the Queen Anne style, one of the most ornate modes. The building now houses a guesthouse. *Courtesy of the History Department, May Hill Russell Library, Key West.*

The Cornish Memorial AME Zion Church on Whitehead Street is the oldest historically black congregation in Key West. With the changing role of religion in modern life, preserving historic buildings such as this can be challenging. *702 Whitehead Street. Courtesy of the History Department, May Hill Russell Library, Key West.*

The Monroe County Courthouse at 500 Whitehead Street is one of a handful of brick government buildings in Key West. Although expensive, masonry is resistant to termites, rot and fire. *Courtesy of the History Department, May Hill Russell Library, Key West.*

This tall wood-frame house is an example of the Queen Anne style at 701 Division Street, now called Truman Avenue, an area developed after the Civil War. *Courtesy of the History Department, May Hill Russell Library, Key West.*

Charles and Sarah Curry built this house at 227 Duval Street around 1874. Charles was the eldest son of millionaire William Curry. Later, the house passed to daughter Carinne Curry, who married Dr. Joseph Fogarty. Today it is a restaurant and bar. *Courtesy of the History Department, May Hill Russell Library, Key West.*

Another son and daughter-in-law of William Curry—Robert and Mercedes—built this Queen Anne style house at 313 Duval Street around 1890. Later, the building served as the headquarters of the Elks Club. It now houses the Hard Rock Café. *Courtesy of the History Department, May Hill Russell Library, Key West.*

The youngest daughter of William Curry, Florida Curry, and her husband, J. Vining Harris, built the Southernmost House at 1400 Duval Street in 1899. It is one of the best examples of the Queen Anne style in Key West. During the 1940s the house became a gambling club. *Courtesy of the History Department, May Hill Russell Library, Key West.*

What is now called the Curry Mansion at 511 Caroline Street was the home of Milton and Elaine Curry. They acquired his parents' house, incorporating a portion of the old house in the rear and building an imposing new front at the turn of the last century. *Courtesy of the History Department, May Hill Russell Library, Key West.*

This house at 703 Fleming Street is one of a pair at the corner of Elizabeth Street. Broadway producer and lyricist Jerry Herman and his partner Marty Finkelstein restored them both. *Courtesy of the History Department, May Hill Russell Library, Key West.*

This wood-frame church, Sparks Chapel, is shown before and after the hurricane of October 11, 1909. Dissenting Methodists originally founded the congregation. They rebuilt after the storm, using poured reinforced concrete. *Courtesy of the History Department, May Hill Russell Library, Key West.*

The same hurricane destroyed the Ruy Lopez cigar factory, shown in this dramatic diptych. Large buildings such as cigar factories and churches fared particularly poorly during a spate of early twentieth-century storms. *Courtesy of the History Department, May Hill Russell Library, Key West.*

The Monroe County courthouse sustained damage during a hurricane in 1919. The walls were subsequently repaired, and buttresses were added to guard against future storms. *Courtesy of the History Department, May Hill Russell Library, Key West.*

This concrete cigar factory was built after a fire destroyed an earlier wood-frame building. During World War II, the navy took over the structure for use as a barracks and cafeteria. It became county and state offices half a century later. *Gato Cigar Factory. Courtesy of the History Department, May Hill Russell Library, Key West.*

This unusual coral rock house at Reynolds and South Streets was constructed circa 1909 by the Reverend E.A. Harrison and his son. The front door addresses the corner, and the principal living area is elevated to protect it against flooding from hurricanes. *Courtesy of the History Department, May Hill Russell Library, Key West.*

The Fleming Street Methodist Church was built on the site of Sparks Chapel. The stained-glass windows with pointed arches recall Gothic architecture. *Courtesy of the History Department, May Hill Russell Library, Key West.*

St. Paul's Episcopal Church is the most impressive example of the ecclesiastical use of the Gothic Revival style. This is the fourth church on the site, shown here under construction circa 1918 with a navy blimp overhead. *Courtesy of the History Department, May Hill Russell Library, Key West.*

Pigeon Key served as a construction and maintenance camp for the Overseas Railway, completed in 1912. Following a devastating hurricane in 1935, the right-of-way was converted to the Overseas Highway, shown here upon its opening in 1938. *Seven Mile Bridge and Pigeon Key. Courtesy of the History Department, May Hill Russell Library, Key West.*

The Hotel Casa Marina was built by a sister company to the railway, as capitalist Henry Flagler considered them to be mutually beneficial businesses. The Mediterranean Revival style was popular because of its associations with posh European resorts. *Courtesy of the History Department, May Hill Russell Library, Key West.*

The Hotel La Concha from 1926 is the tallest commercial building in Old Town Key West. It exemplifies the promise of tourism during the 1920s. It is also in the Mediterranean Revival style. *Courtesy of the History Department, May Hill Russell Library, Key West.*

The Strand Theater on Duval Street was originally constructed circa 1920. This photo shows the building on its first birthday when *The Man from Lost River* was playing. *Courtesy of the History Department, May Hill Russell Library, Key West.*

Expatriate Cubans founded the San Carlos Institute in 1871, although the current building dates to 1924, exhibiting a rich Baroque Revival style. For a while, the building housed the Palace Theater, although it has since been restored to its earlier design. *Courtesy of the History Department, May Hill Russell Library, Key West.*

The Strand Theater experienced substantial remodeling in 1926–27, when a Spanish architect completely redesigned the façade. The building currently houses a chain drugstore. *Strand Theater on 529 Duval Street. Courtesy of the History Department, May Hill Russell Library, Key West.*

ND
ENJOY
TOP
Entertainment
HERE

The cornerstone of the Reynolds School was laid in 1927. Housing the original Monroe County kindergarten, it features ochre-colored brick and copper roofing. *Courtesy of the History Department, May Hill Russell Library, Key West.*

Richard Heyman made national news in 1983 when, as an openly gay man, voters elected him mayor of Key West. The gay community played an important role in rediscovering and restoring historic buildings in town. *Courtesy of the History Department, May Hill Russell Library, Key West.*

Red Cross Houses

Let us examine a group of storm-resistant houses constructed in the Upper Keys nearly seventy years ago.

The scene was Upper Matecumbe and Plantation Key immediately following the devastating hurricane of Labor Day, 1935. One of the most powerful storms ever to hit the United States had just cut its destructive path, killing hundreds of people and destroying scores of houses.

The need for new shelter was acute, but a new and painful awareness of the danger of hurricanes signaled a break with previous building traditions. Although earlier structures were light, wood-frame buildings placed on stone piers, storm survivors were ready for a different approach.

Concrete had been around since ancient times, but in its naturally occurring form it was rare and consequently little used. Only with the Industrial Revolution and the invention of Portland cement was it possible to conceive of whole buildings made of inexpensive poured concrete. By the early twentieth century, factories, mills and other industrial, commercial and institutional buildings utilized the new material.

Following the desolation of the 1935 hurricane, it seemed like a good material for houses in the Florida Keys, too. The American Red Cross and the Federal Emergency Relief Administration developed a series of prototypical one-story homes engineered with hurricanes in mind. For those who owned their own land, one-, two-, three- and four-bedroom designs were available.

The foundation consisted of a massive perimeter wall, sunk solidly into the ground to anchor the structure on a secure footing. Within, a cistern stored water, still a necessary feature before the pipeline brought fresh water to the Keys during the Second World War.

The main floor—also of concrete—was substantially elevated, although not as much as the "stilt" houses that would follow later. Massive walls were a foot thick, glazed with windows using glass reinforced with wire mesh. The roof, too, was concrete, so that it could not peel off. Inside, the electrical outlets were mounted high above the floor, out of the way of potential floodwaters. The resulting structure could potentially withstand whatever Mother Nature might throw at it.

In all, over two dozen of these hurricane houses were built in the Upper Keys, mostly on Upper Matecumbe Key, Plantation Key and Tavernier. For decades, they have provided secure homes for their inhabitants.

While their massive construction would seem to militate against their loss, they face their own kind of preservation challenges.

As moisture creeps into porous concrete, salts crystallize and steel reinforcing rod rusts. This causes spalling, or the spontaneous breaking apart of the aggregate. Repairing such damage can involve jackhammering out crumbling material, replacing rebar and pouring new concrete.

Red Cross houses are not immune from demolition, either. One was torn down in 1970 to make way for the Plantation Yacht Harbor—now Islamorada's Founders' Park. Another one was demolished in 1996 following a long period of decline. Currently, no legal protections are in place to prevent others from being lost, too. Consequently, posterity is relying on their owners to recognize the significance of these unique structures and to maintain them long into the future.

These houses remain as a fascinating example of house design tailored to hurricane threats in the Florida Keys.

For more information, go to www.keyshistory.org.

Historic Wood Construction

Most old buildings in the Keys are wooden, a fact that the inventory of historic buildings in Key West underscores, listing over 2,300 frame structures. Despite any apparent uniformity, however, these buildings have marked differences, spanning and embodying a remarkable period of change and development in construction techniques.

The earliest buildings employed post and beam framing, also known as post-and-girt, timber frame or heavy timber construction. Carpenters used large framing members, hand-hewn or sawn, joining them together with carved joints and wooden pegs. Derived from medieval carpentry traditions, this method saw use among the early settlers to the New World. Later generations moving to Key West in the early nineteenth century erected the first buildings—such as the Oldest House and the Audubon House—using this pre-industrial system.

Serving as bones or inner support structure, framing also affected the outward forms of buildings. Stout posts clearly defining the four corners favored regular, boxy massing, while intermediate supports dividing walls and roofs into structural bays forced doors, windows and dormers between them, giving order and rhythm to the façade.

A second framing system resulted from the advent of the Industrial Revolution, using two new developments in wood-frame construction: cheap nails and standardized lumber. Mass-produced cut nails, evenly tapered from head to point with a rectangular profile, were the first fruits of the mechanized manufacturing of building materials. Later, the invention of the circular saw led to faster cutting of timber into regular sizes, such as two-by-fours.

For much of the nineteenth century, carpenters were reluctant to part entirely with traditional post and beam construction, retaining heavy timbers for corner posts and other significant structural elements. At the same time, they used the new milled lumber and cheap nails in walls for inserting studs between principal posts, in roofing as light rafters between heavy timber trusses and in flooring as joists.

Many mid-nineteenth-century buildings in Key West employed this transitional construction system—halfway between handcraftsmanship and the Industrial Revolution—often exhibiting the popular Greek or Classical Revival style of architecture.

By the end of the nineteenth century, however, the new products of technology and industry took over completely, resulting in a third system. The balloon frame completely dispensed with heavy timbers, employing instead light standardized lumber throughout the structure. Emerging first in rapidly developing Chicago in the 1830s, it eventually spread to all areas of the country.

Nail making changed, too, as manufacturers extruded wire to make the penny fasteners we know today, having flat heads, straight shafts, pointed tips and round cross sections.

With these new developments, the form of buildings changed, sometimes dramatically. With no ponderous posts at corners, many carpenters abandoned the box, instead using light framework to fashion complex, asymmetrical and irregular plans and façades. Furthermore, the lack of big timbers at intermediate locations erased the need for structural bays, allowing greater freedom in the placement of doors, windows and dormers.

Many elaborate Queen Anne style buildings made full use of these new opportunities, such as the Artist House on Eaton Street, featuring an octagonal corner turret, and the Patterson-Spottswood House on Caroline Street, sporting one of the most imaginative façades in Key West. Both houses would have been very difficult and expensive to frame with heavy timbers and hand-carved wooden joints.

By the early twentieth century, tastes reverted to simpler forms, but the new building methods were here to stay. Bungalows found in Tavernier, Pigeon Key and Key West follow contemporary standardized practices.

Wooden buildings in the Keys bridge some of the most significant changes affecting construction technology. Understanding these developments makes it easier to appreciate the skill and workmanship that went into crafting such an important part of the architectural heritage of Monroe County.

Traditional Building Woods

With so many of the Keys's buildings traditionally constructed of wood, many people are interested in learning about the kind of wood used and where it came from. At the same time, few researchers of Keys's structures have performed scientific identification of wood to provide reliable information. Consequently, we must piece together this history based on knowledge of botany, woodworking and economics. Here is one interpretation.

Early settlers in south Florida could make use of several different species of wood suitable for building—some nearby, some farther away.

The closest and most common was south Florida slash pine (*Pinus elliottii densa*), also known as "Dade County" pine. In the Lower Keys, it flourished in the thin soil found on top of Miami oolite capstone. Heavy, dense, hard and termite resistant, it saw common usage here as long as it was available. Scattered stands are still found on Big Pine Key, No Name Key, Little Pine Key, Cudjoe Key and Sugarloaf Key as well as on the mainland from Volusia to Levy County.

During the second half of the nineteenth century, however, a variety of factors worked together to make importing timber increasingly more attractive. Supply and demand surely played a role, as increasing population and the need for wood eventually depleted convenient local supplies of usable timber.

Meanwhile, in Pensacola and other Gulf Coast ports, the timber exporting industry grew rapidly following the Civil War, with lumber barons quickly expanding the infrastructure of this business and looking for new markets.

Additionally, changes in transportation technology—most notably the increasing use of steamships—made importation of all products a more reliable commercial venture.

Three woods not native to the Keys saw widespread exportation from Southern ports:

North American bald cypress, which grows in wet, swampy areas such as the Everglades and the Mississippi Delta, evolved in a harsh environment where survival required continual resistance to moisture-induced decay. Consequently, builders especially valued this wood for exposed exterior uses, such as shingles, shutters and porches.

Cedar, known in the South as juniper, also boasted insect- and fungus-resistant qualities. With the additional benefit of softness and lightness, it saw use traditionally for shingles and for boat building.

Yellow pine, a hard, resinous wood, commonly served in heavy construction work, such as flooring, docks and warehouses.

Besides these Gulf Coast imports, suppliers by the end of the nineteenth century may have begun importing Dade County pine from mainland south Florida, as forests there became accessible to commercial exploitation. The building of port facilities, mills and roads in the 1890s made these previously inaccessible stands of timber available for cutting. By the end of the 1920s, lumbermen depleted the existing supplies, effectively eliminating Dade County pine as a commercially harvestable wood.

We sometimes hear references to "heart" wood or "heart" pine, which describes not so much a species as its place in the tree. It comes from the inner core of the trunk rather than the outer sapwood. Composed of hard deadwood, it is more resistant to decay and termites than the soft, living tissue nearer the bark. Heartwood often contains natural chemicals that contribute to this resistance to insect and fungal attack.

Clearly, more research remains to be done on this topic. Physically verifying the identity of different woods will provide more answers. With an understanding of cellular structure and graining patterns, researchers can examine actual samples from historic buildings under a magnifier or microscope to determine the species and perhaps the origin of woods traditionally used in the Florida Keys.

Sources:
Godwin, Diana Jarvis, "Southern Softwoods," *Old-House Journal*, March–April 1992.
Hardin, E. Dennis, "Pinelands," *The Monroe County Environmental Story* (Big Pine Key: Monroe County Environmental Education Task Force, 1991).
Hoadley, R. Bruce, *Identifying Wood: Accurate Results with Simple Tools* (Taunton Press, 1991).
Pinus elliottii, Center for Wood Anatomy Research, Forest Products Laboratory, USDA Forest Service, Technology Transfer Fact Sheet.

Preserving Historic Masonry

While most old buildings in Key West are wood, the approximately one hundred historic structures of masonry are also significant, employing this more expensive, noncombustible and termite-proof material. They also pose preservation challenges substantially different from other materials.

Masonry construction involves laying up structures of earthen units, such as stone, brick or concrete block and holding them together with mortar.

Masonry work first appears in Key West for fireplaces and chimneys in kitchen outbuildings (such as the one behind the Oldest House). Cisterns, too, required masonry.

Early settlers in the Lower Keys found no clay for bricks and no granite, sandstone or marble. Instead, they met with oolitic limestone, a rock that is crumbly or friable. Perhaps the oldest surviving building employing this material is the Tift and Company Ships Chandlery on Wall Street (now occupied by the Chamber of Commerce). Other buildings employing local stone included the Tift (Hemingway) House, the "Old Stone" Methodist Church and the Convent of Mary Immaculate (now demolished).

Brick first appeared in Key West during the 1840s, especially in government defensive works like Fort Taylor and commercial buildings such as warehouses. Early bricks were handmade and imported by sea. Following the 1886 fire, the need for nonflammable structures resulted in more brick buildings springing up, such as the Harbor House on Front Street. Patrons and builders may also have favored brick for its association with fashionable architecture. By the end of the nineteenth century, a few private houses—like the one the Key West Woman's Club currently occupies—employed brick construction. By this time, too, technology had advanced, making available hard, uniform, machine-made bricks, visible in the Southernmost House and the old First National (now Wachovia) Bank.

Mortar traditionally employed lime, an essential material forming the binding agent for pre-industrial mortar. Workers made quicklime by heating limestone in a kiln. Slaking it with water, they added sand to make mortar.

With the widespread availability of Portland cement, the composition of mortar changed, utilizing this new material in place of most of the lime. This substitution resulted in a harder, stronger mortar.

Before long, builders realized that they could use cement to make not only mortar but also whole blocks, often cast with a rough, ornamental surface resembling stone. Examples locally employing this new material include the old firehouse at Virginia and Grinnell Streets, a row of houses on the 400 block of South Street and the cigar factory and cottages on Staples Avenue near the High School.

For today's property owner or builder, masonry construction presents a number of preservation issues. For early structures, repointing with appropriate mortar is particularly important. The inadvertent use of modern mortars containing high levels of cement can harm old brick. Normal temperature variations cause masonry to expand and contract, action resulting in damaging stresses with incompatible materials. Older and softer handmade bricks surrounded by hard mortar are liable to break apart. A good rule of thumb is that mortar should always be softer than the bricks it binds. An analysis of historic mortar can determine its composition, so that new mortar can match the physical properties of the old.

Other concerns are aesthetic. Historic mortars may be white, like lime, or pigmented, creating a color scheme complementary to brickwork. In such settings, gray, cement-colored mortar invariably stands out. Taking care to match the historic mortar color can forestall this unfortunate effect.

Old brick itself has properties to keep in mind. Historic, kiln-fired brick has a weather-resistant face that can stand up to centuries of exposure. Sandblasting to remove old paint erodes this weather-resistant crust, leaving old brick more vulnerable to weathering. Instead, cleaning and stripping efforts, if undertaken at all, should use the gentlest means possible. Additionally, coatings and sealants applied with the best of intentions may only result in trapping moisture in rather than keeping it out.

For ornamental concrete block, matching roughcast surfaces may be a challenge, as they are not like modern flat-faced concrete blocks. Sensitivity to decorative qualities, however, combined with a high level of craftsmanship can bring out concrete's best qualities, forming as much a part of the architectural heritage of the Keys as other masonry structures.

Historic Roofing Materials

Having a roof over one's head is vitally important to most of us. The obvious practical function of keeping the rain out makes the roof an essential part of every building. Roofing materials also factor into the historic and aesthetic character of many structures. A well-maintained roof contributes to these qualities, while a neglected one can detract from them.

During most of the nineteenth century, builders used wood shingles, which were lightweight, comparatively cheap and easy to ship. Before the Industrial Revolution, workers found wood to be a familiar and low-tech material that they could easily work with hand tools. The cookhouse or kitchen outbuilding behind the Oldest House has a wood roof, as does an unoccupied structure on the 600 block of Louisa Street.

Wood shingles had their drawbacks, however, especially in a town of wood-frame buildings set close together with a limited supply of water for fighting fires. In fact, this proved to be a recipe for disaster, as fires struck Key West in 1843, 1859, 1886 and 1923. Flames leapt from building to building, while embers rained down on neighboring structures, setting them on fire. In desperate attempts to control these blazes, some citizens blew up buildings to create firebreaks, efforts that sometimes resulted in fatal accidents.

Soon, everybody recognized the need for fireproof roofing. Key West's first fire codes mandated it west of Greene Street, and property owners and builders searched for alternative materials.

By the 1890s, a few significant government structures, such as the City Hall, the Lighthouse Keepers Quarters and the Armory, sported slate roofs. During the next four decades, Spanish and Mediterranean style buildings, like First National Bank, the Casa Marina and some houses, featured clay tile roofs.

Both slate and tile roofs are generally very long lasting, enduring for centuries with very little maintenance, but they are also heavy, adding substantial shipping costs to already expensive materials. Their weight may pose installation difficulties, too, especially when retrofitting existing structures not constructed to carry such a load. A further disadvantage of tile is its brittle nature, fracturing under the feet of careless workers. Finally, high winds can blow off slates and tiles, requiring careful installation in hurricane-prone areas such as the Keys.

The vast majority of homeowners needed a more practical material—something cheaper, lighter and more easily installed. Metal shingles answered this need and became very common. Engineers developed them in France during the 1870s, making them of sheet iron or steel and stamping or embossing them with patterns. Lead, tin, zinc or an alloy of tin and lead known as terne coated all surfaces with a weather-resistant, non-ferrous, non-rusting finish. The edges of each shingle linked to its neighbors to reinforce each other and prevent the wind from lifting them. When installed together on a roof, they resulted in a shimmering, fish scale pattern.

Roofs are likely to experience two different kinds of problems—with the shingles themselves or with fastenings. The exposed outer coatings of shingles are vulnerable to gradual erosion, permitting water to reach the core metal, causing rust to bleed through and streak the surface. If left unchecked, rust will eat through a roof just the way it can damage a car. The recommended treatment is relatively simple: chemically treat rust to arrest its growth, prime and paint.

Additionally, shingles that are in otherwise good condition are liable to come loose if nails are too rusted, too small or too few in number to adequately hold shingles in place. Not surprisingly, high winds will test this.

Replacement materials, if needed, should be visually similar to those used historically. Heavy-gauge shingles will last considerably longer than thinner material. A conscientious roofer carefully following the building code should not scrimp on fastenings.

If adequately maintained, historic metal shingle roofs will last a very long time. Some installations on Key West houses are over one hundred years old.

Preserving Historic Windows

Windows are among the most significant features of historic buildings, playing a key role in defining the character of traditional vernacular architecture. Appropriate windows immediately distinguish a well-preserved structure, while inappropriate ones can visibly detract from it.

The first windows in pioneer buildings in the Keys consisted merely of openings flanked by board and batten shutters with no glass. As soon as resources permitted, however, settlers battling rain, wind and mosquitoes imported glass, virtually essential for a window as we know it.

Before the mid-nineteenth century, glassmakers worked by hand, carefully heating sand and alkali in a furnace to produce the molten material that was blown, flattened and cut to form panes. Tiny air bubbles and the necessarily small scale of the finished product are the chief characteristics of this expensive and labor-intensive process.

Carpenters then built wood sash and muntins, planing each of these elements by hand and joining them together with pegged mortise and tenon joints. They mounted the panes in the sash, holding them in place from the outside with glazing points and putty. Two sashes of six panes each composed a typical double hung window, with the upper sash sometimes fixed in place.

The openings themselves display the proportions of a vertical rectangle, with a height at least twice the width and sometimes as much as three times the width. Early designers typically spaced these openings regularly across the façade of a building, with upstairs and downstairs window openings in alignment with each other or with doorways. This attention to proportion, rhythm and harmony contributes to the beauty and charm of many old buildings.

As the nineteenth century progressed, industrial techniques developed to make larger sheets of smoother glass at a lower cost. Builders consequently made sash with fewer, larger panes. Additionally, they fitted sashes with counterweights and cords or chains to make them easier to open and close. By the early twentieth century, casement windows with wood sash hinged on each side appeared in some buildings such as bungalows.

Jalousie and awning windows came into production in the mid-twentieth century, utilizing manufactured metal and glass. They have the advantage of opening more completely and having no wood to feed termites. Yet they are usually not appropriate on earlier buildings, having wider, squatter proportions that often necessitated altering the original openings. Moreover, newer windows with metal louvers or frosted jalousies effectively block the opening when closed. They also lack the craftsmanship of real wood windows.

Historic wood windows in good condition are important survivals and keeping them painted and puttied will help preserve them. Those showing termite damage, weathering or wear are better repaired than replaced, if possible. Typical repair can involve taking out the sashes, patching damaged wood with new wood or epoxy consolidant and replacing broken panes, lost putty and worn sash cords.

If total replacement is the only option, new wood sashes that are visually similar to historic materials will be the most appropriate. Both the proportion of the window opening and the orientation of the panes should emphasize the vertical axis. Furthermore, narrow muntins with delicate moldings are typical of nineteenth-century windows. Finally, each pane should be individually glazed in putty and made of clear, untinted glass.

Information about suppliers of historically appropriate windows can be found by consulting the Old House Journal's Restoration Directory (www.oldhousejournal.com) or an architect with experience in historic preservation.

A Short History of Nails

Now an inexpensive and common building article, nails at one time were expensive and scarce. Different kinds of nails show the evolution of technology and the advance of the Industrial Revolution. Based upon such changes, nails may also help date old buildings.

Nails divide into three overlapping types and phases: hand-wrought nails, cut nails and wire nails.

For centuries, blacksmiths, nailers and farmers made nails by hand one at a time on an anvil. They began with a long iron rod, square in section and approximately ¼ inch thick. After heating one end in a forge, they hammered each of the four sides to a tapering point, broke it off and placed it upright in a hole. By hammering the projecting end to spread it out, artisans created a "rose," "butterfly" or L-head. This slow and labor-intensive process resulted in costly products, which prudent builders reused when practical to do so.

Indeed, to minimize the need for iron nails, the art of wood joinery developed, enjoying high status among the crafts. Master craftsmen created hand-cut joints held together with wooden pegs or "treenails." This system saw use in building frames of ships, furniture and houses, including early wood buildings in the Keys.

Due to the high cost of hand-wrought nails, inventors diligently tried to develop cheaper ways of production. As a result, this craft experienced some of the earliest innovations of the Industrial Revolution in the United States, and the nail industry grew quickly with the development of cut nails.

Manufacturers made cut nails by placing an iron bar on a flat iron surface with the end of the bar overhanging the edge of the surface. A heavy hammer then slammed straight down onto the projecting end of the bar, breaking it off. The lower edge where the break occurred left a rough edge or burr, which may still be detected by running one's finger across the edge. To make tapered nails, the bar was placed at a slight angle from perpendicular to the edge of the working surface; but unlike handmade nails, they are tapered on two sides only, with the other two sides being parallel.

Early cut nails (1790s–1820s) still had handmade heads, showing them to be transitional between craft and industrial modes of production. A few examples of these nails exist in Key West, probably recycled from earlier buildings.

By 1830, it became practical to make heads by machine. For the next fifty years, cut nails dominated the field.

Yet handmade nails were not obsolete, since cut nails tended to be too brittle for some uses. By contrast, hand hammering on a forge produced a strong, high-quality iron that resisted rust and could be clinched. Consequently, hand-forged nails continued in use for a while with gates, doors, wagons and boats.

Meanwhile, a third way to make nails was emerging. Manufacturers in the United States experimented with utilizing extruded wire, rather than rolled bar stock, to make wire nails in the 1850s. These came into greater production by the 1870s.

During the 1880s other new developments took place. The Bessemer process for making steel began to affect the making of nails, and by the end of that decade, most nails were steel.

In 1886 the production of cut nails in the United States reached a peak of over eight million kegs. Yet at the same time, 10 percent of the market lay in the new wire nails. In that year, Key West experienced a devastating fire, and structures rebuilt following this disaster probably reflect the prevalence of these types of nails.

By the 1890s, sales of wire nails surpassed cut nails, and by 1913, wire nails composed more than 90 percent of total production.

Incidentally, nails are classified by size based upon the ancient price for a hundred count. For example, ten-penny nails originally cost ten pence (written 10d) per hundred. Although prices have changed, the classification system remains as an indicator of size: 2d nails are 1 inch long; 8d nails are 2½ inches long; and 100d nails are 8-inch spikes.

We may take nails for granted today, but they were the subject of centuries of painstaking invention and development. The different kinds of nails bear witness to these changes and can help us track the unique evolution of our historic buildings.

A Brief History of Paint

Paint is one of the most frequently asked about topics in preservation, often playing a highly visible role in the presentation of historic buildings to the public. The use of paint reflects historical trends, while its inevitable deterioration and periodic renewal raise contemporary concerns.

Paint consists of a liquid medium, usually oil or water, and pigment. Oil paints traditionally used boiled linseed oil, shifting later to petroleum distillates. Oil paint of high quality is weather-resistant, wearing well in adverse conditions. Early water-based paints—like whitewash made with quicklime and whiting—are cheaper, traditionally requiring annual renewal.

Technology, economics and fashion have affected the history of paint.

The availability of naturally occurring pigments limited the range of the early color palette. Craftsmen used white lead, iron oxide, ochre, verdigris and soot, mixing paints by hand.

The earliest buildings in the Keys were probably unpainted, as paint was a luxury that struggling settlers could dispense with. Even in later times, poorer households did without.

When resources permitted, however, property owners sought to follow current fashions. In the first half of the nineteenth century, white (utilizing lead carbonate) reigned supreme as the most popular color, while green for shutters played a notable supporting role. Observers commented on this color scheme in all areas of the country. Gleaming white marble ruins in Greece inspired a mania for classical architecture, prompting many to mimic its austere, sun-bleached qualities.

By the middle of the nineteenth century, a rebellion against the widespread use of white was growing. Alexander Jackson Downing promoted the Gothic Revival style, based on medieval architecture having soft earth tones. Fawn, drab, gray and brown came into vogue.

By the late nineteenth century, advances in chemistry paved the way for a broad selection of colors, and new companies produced ready-mixed paint by the 1870s. Many consumers employed darker colors, such as brown, olive and red, painting their elaborate Victorian buildings with contrasting schemes, highlighting individual architectural elements in different hues.

The twentieth century brought a return to the past. Colonial Revivalists favored traditional ochre or white, the latter sometimes employing zinc instead of lead. Later, the hard times of the Depression resulted in less painting altogether. Further developments in chemistry during the 1950s led to the use of titanium dioxide in white paint and the emergence of latex paints.

Paint failure comes in many forms. Cracking, flaking, peeling, blistering, checking, alligatoring and crazing may be symptomatic of a variety of problems. Ultraviolet light, water, aging and the incompatibility of different paint layers cause specific troubles. For example, simple aging often results in chalking and small flakes, while moisture under the surface of paint tends to produce peeling in large sheets.

Repainting poses a number of questions, the first of which may be the search for an appropriate color. A qualified architectural conservator can determine the historic color of a building by taking paint samples, viewing them under a microscope and subjecting them to chemical tests. Lacking this, one may select a color based on the architectural style and period of the building.

In preparing for painting, it is best to utilize the gentlest means possible, such as scraping and sanding or, if necessary, pressure washing below six hundred pounds per square inch. To be avoided are sandblasting (which erodes the surface of wood, leaving a rough texture of ridges and furrows), blowtorches (a notorious fire hazard) and rotary drill attachments (which can irreversibly damage wood).

With an understanding of how people used paint in the past along with knowledge of how to maintain paint today, we can preserve historic buildings for the future.

Preserving Historic Interiors

Although the exteriors of old buildings are often the subject of careful consideration during rehabilitation—since they are visible to the public and frequently subject to review by local preservation commissions—interiors also form a part of the overall significance of a historic property and should be preserved wherever possible.

It is not uncommon to hear those who have recently acquired a historic building say, "What a charming old house! Now we're just going to gut it..." apparently unaware of the contradictory impulses involved. By the time the oversize dumpster arrives on the sidewalk to be filled with the contents of the building this philosophy of destroy and rebuild is being translated into reality.

Interiors can be seen from the macro to the micro. The largest aspect is the plan, or sequence of rooms and spaces. Next in scale are rooms and spaces themselves, particularly their size and proportion. At the closest level of detail are the decorative elements and finishes.

The plan determines the organization of spaces in a building and often reflects historical traditions of building and design. Many of the earliest houses in Key West, for example, have a center-hall plan, consisting of a symmetrical arrangement of rooms on either side of a stair hall running the depth of the house, allowing for the unimpeded circulation of air and people.

After the middle of the nineteenth century, other houses featured a side-hall plan, an asymmetrical layout with the stair hall placed to one side and a double-parlor on the other. Almost invariably, a smaller addition to the rear houses the kitchen and other service rooms.

A third category of historic plan is found in many of Key West's one-story cigar makers' cottages, which naturally dispense with a staircase, while elongating the sequence of rooms into a distinctively long and linear format that suits the Island City's narrow city lots.

In addition to the plan, a building's interior is also affected by the size, scale and proportion of rooms and other interior spaces. Stair halls are often the most dramatic interior spaces of old houses, rising through two or even three stories. High ceilings also frequently characterize rooms designed for warm weather. Earlier and simpler rooms may have harmonious rectangular or square proportions, while late Victorian spaces may boast complex bays and niches that reflect that period's interest in varied and interesting interior spaces.

Finally, interior trim and finishes contribute to the historic character of old buildings. Even the simplest of Key West houses may sport what in many other locations would seem to be a lavish use of wood for floors, walls and ceilings. Doors and windows as well as their casings or moldings can be simple or elaborate, but either way, they too speak to a building's past. Ornate staircases, painted ceilings, decorative columns and even fireplaces, though unusual, gain significance from their very rarity.

Of course, in a regrettable number of cases, alterations have already seriously compromised the historic integrity of interiors, whether through inappropriate additions or subtractions. Subsequent add-ons, such as dividing walls, dropped ceilings, wall coverings and linoleum floors can often be removed to reveal the earlier material.

Dealing with the loss of historic interior elements may present more of a challenge. Where adequate documentary, pictorial or physical evidence is present, it may be possible to restore these lost features. Lacking adequate evidence one may be left guessing, subject to the vagaries of conjecture. In such cases, a well-designed, harmonious, contemporary treatment may be appropriate.

With an understanding of how the interior of an old building contributes to its overall historical significance, one can design and execute a sensitive rehabilitation that respects the past, provides enjoyment in the present and preserves our architectural heritage for the future.

For more information, see *Preservation Brief 18*, "Rehabilitating Interiors in Historic Buildings" by H. Ward Jandl, published by the Preservation Assistance Division of the National Park Service (on the web at www2.cr.nps.gov/tps/briefs/brief18.htm).

Historic Keys Furnishings

How were houses in the Keys furnished historically? Answering this question requires some inquiry into settlement patterns, shipping routes, technological developments and changing fashions.

Before the Civil War, most settlers came here from the Bahamas and the eastern seaboard of the United States. For example, a number of early families have documented origins in Nassau, Green Turtle Cay, Connecticut, New York and South Carolina. Additionally, during the last third of the nineteenth century, Cuban immigration increased significantly, forming a direct link to Havana. No doubt many of these new arrivals brought some household furnishings with them from these places of origin.

Shipping and transportation enters into the equation as well, especially for consumers buying imported goods. Key West had the distinction of being an official port of entry, giving it a privileged position in obtaining goods from abroad. Additionally, in the antebellum years, regular sailing and steamship service connected Key West to such furniture-making centers as Charleston and New Orleans; in the years following the Civil War, scheduled routes expanded to include Baltimore, Havana and New York. By 1912, the Florida East Coast Railway had completed the Key West Extension, providing a new way to bring in goods from the mainland.

In considering household furnishings in the Keys, it is also helpful to remember that the Industrial Revolution completely transformed manufacturing during the nineteenth century. Objects that individual artisans had made by hand in small shops increasingly became the product of teams of workers using new machines in larger mills.

Furniture making, for example, had long been the domain of highly skilled cabinetmakers and joiners. By the middle of the nineteenth century, the introduction of new woodworking tools and machines—band saws, circular saws and the like—challenged the old ways, as manufacturers discovered that they could now produce a larger volume of cheaper goods. A number of more recently settled cities, in particular, embraced the new technology, becoming large furniture-making centers.

Fashion is another aspect of household furnishings in the Keys. In the early nineteenth century, the Empire style based on classical forms enjoyed popularity, a natural complement to Key West's Classical Revival houses. By mid-century, elaborate French modes rose to prominence, such as the ornate Rococo Revival, boasting curvilinear forms and elaborate carving made with new woodworking machines.

Other styles multiplied during the Victorian period (1837–1901), frequently based on earlier historical periods: Renaissance Revival, Elizabethan Revival, Gothic Revival, even Egyptian Revival. One English design reformer, Charles Eastlake, lent his name to a style inspired from his writings. By the last quarter of the nineteenth century, the Colonial Revival style looked back to early American history.

During the early twentieth century, a rebellion against this multiplicity of historical styles and cheap, machine-made ornament brought about the Craftsman, Mission or Arts and Crafts style, featuring more "honest," simplified forms. Some of these later kinds of furniture were available through mail order catalogues such as Sears, Roebuck, and Company.

Because of all these forces, interiors in the Keys probably had an exceptionally eclectic mix of furnishings. Residents may have owned a combination of family pieces from their ancestral homes, objects shipped for sale here from a variety of East and Gulf Coast ports, older handmade pieces and newer machine-made objects: all in the profusion of popular styles that flourished between the early nineteenth and the mid-twentieth centuries.

Historic homes in Key West open to the public offer an opportunity for further study. The Oldest House features a variety of representative objects from the nineteenth century. The Audubon House boasts an especially fine, high-style collection. The Lighthouse Keepers Quarters are furnished in an austere, homey fashion appropriate to their historic function. Twentieth-century residents distinguished the Heritage House, the Hemingway House and Truman Little White House, although their collections often look back to earlier styles.

With a greater understanding of the history of settlement, transportation, technology and taste—and by examining existing interiors one can better visualize how householders furnished their homes in the Keys.

Fires and Historic Buildings

Fires have had an unmistakable impact on historic buildings, periodically destroying individual landmarks or sweeping through entire neighborhoods. Though rebuilding heals these wounds superficially, scars nevertheless remain, testifying to traumatic events affecting both what is lost and what is rebuilt.

The vanished settlement at Indian Key is a striking example of the power of fire. Founded in 1830 as a wrecking port that could compete with Key West, it fell victim to a raid during the Second Seminole War ten years later. A war party of over one hundred men burnt thirty-eight buildings, including houses, kitchens, shops and warehouses. Following a brief military occupation, the island was permanently abandoned. Currently preserved as an archaeological site, it remains a silent witness of its disastrous history.

Key West, though never wiped out by fire, has certainly suffered from its devastating effects, beginning in 1843 when a waterfront warehouse caught fire. A rudimentary fire department possessed a hand-pumping fire engine, which historian Walter Maloney writes "was never of much use and…was entirely neglected…It was brought upon the scene, but proving unfit for use, was contemptuously and indignantly hurled into the sea from the wharf." The flames, which fortunately did not spread to neighboring buildings, eventually exhausted all available fuel.

A bigger blaze in 1859, also in the waterfront district, led one citizen to try a different firefighting technique. Henry Mulrennan took a keg of gunpowder from Fort Taylor, then under construction, and blew up his house at Greene and Fitzpatrick Streets, creating a gap or firebreak to check the spread of flames. This daring strategy proved successful, ultimately saving many buildings, including the nearby Geiger (Audubon) house. Yet an area bounded by Simonton Street, Greene Street and the water lay in ruins.

Key West's worst fire erupted in 1886 at the San Carlos Institute. Loyalists to Spanish rule in Cuba may have ignited the blaze as payback to the Cuban community here, which had supported the Cuban War for Independence. The wind carried the flames block by block all the way to the waterfront. Unfortunately, the City's steam fire engine was in New York for repairs, and attempts to blow up buildings resulted in three deaths. Twelve hours later, the fire burned itself out.

To prevent such a disaster in the future, many replacement buildings west of Greene Street soon employed masonry walls and metal shingle roofs. Meanwhile the City built a system of fire hydrants and pipes fed with seawater.

Smaller fires continued to take their toll. A blaze in 1901 destroyed the first Catholic church of 1852 on Duval Street, near Eaton Street. As a result, St. Mary's relocated to Division Street (Truman Avenue), erecting the concrete church that stands today.

The Gato Cigar Company had a similar experience around 1916, losing a wooden building to a fire and replacing it with a concrete structure. This landmark at the corner of Simonton and Virginia Streets has recently benefited from a substantial rehabilitation.

Other fires read like an obituary column for dead buildings: The White Street fire of 1923 leveled a small neighborhood. A blaze in 1957 consumed the Jefferson Hotel on Duval Street. The Curry & Sons ship chandlery burned in 1963. Outside of Key West, a fire in 1978 destroyed the Big Pine Inn, a well-known landmark since the days of the railroad.

Fortunately, firefighting techniques and fire codes have improved considerably in the last century and a half, developments that one hopes will keep future damage to a minimum. Yet the fires of history have left an indelible mark on the Monroe County we see today.

Hurricanes: Some Lessons from History

Let us take a look at some of the notable storms of the past and examine how people safeguarded their property from these seasonal weather events.

The first wave of settlers to the Keys brought with them construction techniques well suited to the demands of the environment. Employing stout timber construction, they used small shuttered windows and kept houses low, traditionally not higher than 2½ stories. They also built on limestone piers to allow storm surge waters to pass underneath and sheathed interiors in wood, taking a cue from boat- and shipbuilding to add strength.

The first builders sought building sites on comparatively higher ground. They found the greater elevations in Key West on the western side of the island, laying out streets that would later form the heart of Old Town. Those days, safety concerns predominated over the modern obsession for waterfront views.

Structures and sites too near the water soon paid the price for it. The hurricane of October 9–11, 1846, quite vividly demonstrated the dangers of too great a proximity to the ocean, as three examples show:

Government engineers had originally built the first lighthouse on the water at the southern tip of the island to make it more visible from sea. The storm carried it away, along with those who had taken refuge inside it. Subsequently, the Lighthouse Service erected a replacement tower farther inland and on higher ground on Whitehead Street, where it stands today.

The beach on the Atlantic side of the island was another exposed position, where the first settlers buried the dead, relegating this unpleasant need to the outskirts of town. The storm inundated that early cemetery, scattering human remains across the island. City leaders soon selected a new spot near Solares Hill as far inland as possible for its successor, which is still in existence.

A third danger spot also bore the brunt of the 1846 hurricane's fury. Fort Taylor originally stood facing the main shipping channel with the sea lapping right up against its brick walls. The army began construction of the fort in 1845, but the storm set the project back considerably. Work resumed following the storm, although a broad swath of fill now buffers it from the sea.

Thirty years later, another hurricane—on October 19–20, 1876—also demonstrated the vulnerability of certain locations. Most of the damage occurred on the low-lying eastern end of the island, where entrepreneurs were using the salt ponds for a sea salt evaporation industry. The storm washed away fifteen thousand bushels of salt, damaging the works and destroying this industry in Key West.

Besides reminding people of dangerous locations, hurricanes also showed that the roofs of buildings were inherently at risk. Following the 1876 storm, we learned of damage specifically to metal roofs. After the great hurricane of October 11, 1909, we heard a fuller comment on roof damage from historian Jefferson Browne: "Nearly all sheet metal roofs were blown off. Buildings with wooden shingles weathered the storm best, and those with metal shingles next."

Storm surge created another problem that occasionally floated houses off their foundations. This happened in 1846, destroying some buildings entirely. The hurricane of October 17, 1910, washed two houses at the Atlantic end of Duval Street off their foundations onto South Street.

Meanwhile, a trio of hurricanes in the early twentieth century seemed to show the vulnerability of large-scale buildings: The devastating 1909 storm destroyed four cigar factories, an equal number of churches, a firehouse and two stores. Yet another one in 1910 knocked down a cigar factory, the telegraph station and La Brisa "pleasure pavilion." Finally, the 1919 hurricane took out more cigar factories, driving the final nail into the coffin of that industry.

By this time, materials became widely available that would characterize twentieth-century architecture: concrete, usually reinforced with steel. Both ornamental block and poured concrete appeared in new buildings at this time. The Harris School, the Division Street Grammar School, the new St. Paul's Church, the new Fleming Street Church and Trinity Presbyterian Church all utilized this innovative technique.

As we look back over this remarkable history of building and survival, we see an evolution involving both tradition and change. Builders retained the tried-and-true methods of construction they already knew, paying heed to carefully locating site improvements and readily adopting new materials and techniques as they became available.

Hurricanes and Historic Buildings: What Can I Do?

A number of strategies are available for protecting historic buildings from the ravages of tropical storms.

Perhaps the best protection against hurricane damage is regular and timely maintenance. Like disease among a group of living beings, hurricanes are more likely to damage weakened structures. Keeping ahead of termites, rot and other forms of decay can help ensure that buildings retain the structural integrity needed to weather bad storms.

Retrofitting involves going beyond maintenance to alter or add to buildings for greater protection. At their best, such efforts successfully accomplish two different goals, simultaneously preparing old buildings for hurricanes while preserving their unique and irreplaceable historic character.

Retrofitting generally focuses on two complementary strategies: reinforcing the structural frame (the "bones") of a building and reinforcing the weathertight exterior (the "skin") of a structure.

Efforts for reinforcing the frame recognize that buildings require strength in ways not previously taken into account. Traditionally, the emphasis has been on holding buildings *up*, since successfully resisting the inexorable pull of gravity is naturally one of the first principles of structural engineering. But in storm conditions, buildings experience forces from the side or even pulling from above. Consequently, holding buildings *down* becomes important. This realization has resulted in new ways of preventing such uplift.

Uplift connectors provide strength against these forces, holding the frame onto the foundation and connecting all the wooden portions of the frame—sills, studs, plates and rafters—to each other. The result is a strong skeleton that can withstand forces from any direction. Such connectors are mandatory in new construction, and one can also add them to existing historic buildings. The installation of roof connectors in particular can be relatively easy, as unfinished attics provide ready access to exposed timbers.

Sealing up the exterior skin of buildings usually focuses on windows and doors. The traditional approach, of course, involves using wooden shutters, which may be louvered or solid, having hinges either at the top (Bahama-style) or on the sides ("colonial" style). Such shutters have worked well for centuries, and hundreds of buildings in Old Town and throughout the Southeast rely on them.

Another approach involves employing removable plywood storm panels. These may be especially suitable in locations where they can be conveniently reached for installation.

Glazing windows with a stronger material may also work, especially if a building needs new windows anyway. For example, the recently rehabilitated Gato Building on Simonton Street utilizes laminated glass, while the second-floor windows at the Armory on White Street now feature tempered glass. Alternately, historic glass may remain safely in place with an exterior storm window of bulletproof glass (actually a synthetic such as Lexan). St. Paul's Church has protected its magnificent stained glass windows in this way.

Perforated metal screens are another new approach to protecting windows. They will not block wind, but they can stop objects from breaking the glass behind them. Unfortunately, they are expensive and can obscure the view of the windows from the outside. Readers can see for themselves by taking a look at the county courthouse in Jackson Square, which currently sports this new technology.

In addition to these options for retrofitting buildings, attending to landscaping on site is another strategy for reducing damage. Although trees may help block winds, if they stand too close to buildings, they will do far more damage than wind alone. Timely pruning by an arborist can prevent this.

For more information, see the *Hurricane Readiness Guide for Owners and Managers of Historic Resources* by Ellen Uguccioni and Joseph Herndon, a booklet published by the National Trust for Historic Preservation.

FEMA Regulations and Historic Buildings

Buried deep in the heart of arcane federal regulations are some provisions that could be of assistance to you, if you own a historic building that you intend to rehabilitate.

These regulations are found in the dense and wordy rules governing the flood insurance program underwritten by the Federal Emergency Management Agency (FEMA). Since the Keys participate in this essential program, our local building officials must enforce FEMA's mandates. The rationale is that since the federal government is taking the risk of backing our insurance policies, they have a say in what they will insure. Through their regulations, FEMA tries to encourage building practices that will reduce damage claims in the future.

Take elevating buildings, for example. The regulations state that "all new construction and substantial improvements of residential structures" in low-lying areas shall be "elevated to or above the base flood level," the elevation below which there is a 1 percent or greater chance of flooding in any given year. This provision has given rise to the ubiquitous stilt houses that now pepper the landscape of the Keys.

Another means of compliance available for non-residential structures is flood proofing: employing engineering and construction measures designed to reduce damage, even if a building is below base flood level and consequently at higher risk.

Existing buildings, however, only have to fall in line with these requirements if they are subject to "substantial improvements." That is defined as any work on a structure "the cost of which equals or exceeds 50 percent of the market value of the structure." Also known as the "50 percent rule," this infamous imperative triggers a higher—and more expensive—level of compliance.

But here is where it gets interesting for those dealing with preservation projects. The definition of "substantial improvement" specifically excludes "historic structures" from the requirements. Moreover, the regulations state, "variances may be issued for the repair or rehabilitation of historic structures."

These exceptions recognize that today's notions of how to achieve flood safety may not be appropriate for historic buildings. Indeed, one can easily imagine the bizarre streetscape of conch houses on stilts that might result if these provisions did not exist. Moreover, practical experience also plays a role. While computer models, hydrodynamic analysis and flood risk calculations should theoretically point toward reducing damages, many historic buildings have in fact survived a century or more with a number of hurricanes. These rely on careful siting a respectful distance from the sea, comparatively low-rise designs to avoid the worst winds and conservative, sound craftsmanship.

A "historic structure," by the way, is defined as any structure that meets one of the following criteria: individually listed on the National Register of Historic Places, contributing to the historical significance of a registered historic district or listed on a state or local inventory of historic places certified by the Secretary of the Interior.

So the baker's dozen of buildings in Monroe County that are individually listed on the National Register of Historic Places are covered by this definition. Also included are the over 2,500 structures in Key West, over 50 in Tavernier and a dozen more on Pigeon Key that are listed as contributing to certified historic districts. Additionally, buildings outside of designated districts that are included in the historic inventories of Key West or unincorporated Monroe County are covered, since both these jurisdictions have historic preservation programs certified by the Secretary of the Interior.

The FEMA rules have a significant stipulation regarding the kind of work that can be done on historic buildings. Any proposed repair, rehabilitation or alteration must "not preclude the structure's continued historic designation." In other words, you cannot take advantage of this exception to the 50 percent rule—specifically targeted for historic buildings—to do work that would destroy the historic integrity of the building. So for the advantages offered, one must be prepared to bear the obligations, too.

Plodding through long tracts of federal regulations may not be everyone's cup of tea, but an awareness of their mandates and exemptions will make property owners wise to what is required and what is not in the event that major work is undertaken on a historic building.

For more information, see the Code of Federal Regulations, Title 44, Parts 59.1 and 60.6, available online at www.access.gpo.gov/nara/cfr/.

Preservation and the Building Code

Preserving the historic integrity of structures while complying with modern building codes presents a variety of challenges and involves reconciling diverse values.

Most of the historic buildings in the Keys pre-date the advent of modern building codes. During early days, people generally constructed what they wanted. Only in more urban areas, reacting to specific problems, did building codes initially emerge.

Fire precipitated the first codes in many cities, from London to Boston to Key West, which all had initially relied on flammable wood construction. Following the great 1886 fire here, for example, buildings west of Greene Street had to be of masonry with fireproof roofing.

In many other respects, though, government did not regulate most construction practices. It was not until the twentieth century that regional organizations wrote and promulgated the principal building codes in use today, including the Standard Building Code, which emerged in the 1940s and saw widespread adoption throughout the South. The following decade, officials in Dade and Broward Counties developed the South Florida Building Code in an effort to respond to hurricane threats. The state legislature required each local government to adopt a building code by 1984, leaving it up to municipalities to select which code, as long as they met certain minimum standards.

Hurricane Andrew—which struck south Florida in 1992—changed all that. In the wake of that devastating storm, a combination of public outcry, massive insurance losses and scandal involving builders and inspectors led to a complete revamping of the building code in Florida. A statewide Building Commission undertook the project of drafting a consistent building code. A decade later, the new Florida Building Code went into effect.

Not surprisingly, provisions to better secure buildings against hurricanes play a central role in this Code. Additionally, life safety, fire and accessibility codes make further demands. The result is voluminous and comprehensive, regulating egress requirements, stair specifications, railing heights—even the distance around a toilet. All of these minutiae would seem to make it impossible to legally occupy not just a historic building, but any building constructed before the adoption of these requirements.

At the same time, the new Code gives considerable discretion to local building officials in interpreting its mandates. Local authorities may accept "alternate materials and methods" to achieve equivalent effectiveness, fire resistance and safety. This clause represents a different way of thinking about codes, acknowledging that a detailed rulebook (a prescriptive approach) may not be appropriate in all cases. This latitude offers an avenue for accomplishing the objective that everyone wants—safe buildings without absurd regulations.

Regarding historic buildings, the Florida Building Code contains a significant chapter on existing structures. Indeed, it states that compliance with all provisions of the code "shall not be mandatory" for "qualified historic buildings" as long as "such buildings or structures are judged by the building official to be safe and in the public interest of health, safety and welfare." "Qualified historic buildings" are those listed or eligible for listing on the National Register of Historic Places, or those designated locally—either individually or as part of a district. In addition, an appendix to the code includes the "Secretary of the Interior's Standards for Rehabilitation," which form the basis of preservation guidelines across the country.

With this in mind, one can rehabilitate historic buildings, ensuring their safety for future occupancy, while also preserving important features that give them their distinctive character.

For more information on the Florida Building Code, see www.floridabuilding.org.

Termites and Historic Buildings

In a town full of wooden buildings, property owners are naturally concerned about termites. What are these pests, what threat do they pose and how do we stop them?

Termites are an order of over 2,700 species of insects found around the world. Generally, entomologists classify termites according to their mode of living:

Subterranean termites live underground, feeding on wood at ground level or crawling up to available wood, building telltale tunnels on foundation walls to protect themselves while they climb.

Among the most devastating species of subterranean termites are Formosan termites, probably imported accidentally to the United States from Southeast Asia during World War II. More aggressive than their native North American cousins, they have garnered headlines in preservation circles recently due to the threat they pose to the historic wooden buildings of New Orleans. They can also be found elsewhere on the Gulf Coast and even in some parts of Florida.

Dry wood termites live in any deadwood, whether on the ground or far from it. They can fly up to an inviting habitat, and they do not need much moisture to survive and thrive. These are what we predominantly face in the Keys. Two other types, damp wood termites and mound builders, do not live in Florida.

Termites consume wood or cellulose thus performing biologically important work, assisting in the decomposition and recycling of old trees. Unfortunately, termites do not distinguish between deadwood in a forest and timber in a historic building. During the course of their life cycle, they burrow into wood, creating cavities known as galleries, expelling particles of sawdust-like fecal material called frass.

Traditionally, local carpenters utilized indigenous Southern woods, which having evolved here along with termites are comparatively resistant to their voracious appetite. South Florida slash pine (also known as Dade County pine), old-growth North American bald cypress and cedar (known in the South as juniper) are examples.

Nevertheless, old buildings probably have experienced active infestations at some time during their history. Consequently, a property owner today should begin with an inspection to determine whether termite-damaged wood is the result of active or inactive infestation. Look for and remove all visible frass, then wait to see if it returns. If it does not return, termite activity may well have ceased, no longer posing a threat. If it does, termite infestation is probably active.

Stopping an active infestation typically involves tenting structures and releasing fumigants to kill insects. These are invariably highly toxic gasses, necessitating vacating the building of people, pets and food during the procedure. Other treatments for active termite activity include the use of heat, cold, electricity and microwaves.

To prevent re-infestation, a less toxic chemical treatment is seeing increasing use. This involves coating wood with a solution of boric acid. Although this treatment will not eliminate an active termite infestation, it can prevent uninfested wood from coming under attack.

In some cases, buildings may require new wood to replace heavily damaged wood, for new additions or other new construction. Since the most commonly available commercial woods—Douglas fir, hemlock and spruce—are not very termite resistant, they should be treated with chemicals for use in this environment. Most familiar are the green copper arsenic formulations that may be applied by hand or under pressure. The latter is more effective, though not failsafe, since even pressure treatment may only penetrate the outermost ¼ to ½ inch, depending on the porosity of the wood. Additionally, due to the treated wood's toxicity, workers should avoid breathing its sawdust and dispose of scraps carefully.

Alternatively, naturally termite-resistant woods may be used, such as redwood and white oak. Although more expensive than pressure-treated wood, these will retain their natural color, which may be a consideration for fine interior finish work, such as floors, paneling or cabinetry.

Dry Rot and Historic Buildings

Let's talk about rot: specifically dry rot.

Most people have heard of it, although fewer know what it is. We know that natural materials biodegrade over time. But what causes things to rot?

Several species of fungus are responsible: *Merulius lacrymans*, *Poria incrassata* and especially *Serpula lacrymans*.

And in spite of this common syndrome's name, dry rot requires moisture. In wood, the tipping point is a moisture content of about 20 to 30 percent by weight. Normal kiln- or air-dried lumber, when sold, is typically dryer than that. Consequently, wooden buildings and boats are especially subject to dry rot in places that are habitually damp.

An infestation of dry rot begins modestly. Spores are activated by moisture, so areas directly abutting masonry are especially vulnerable, as moisture in the masonry feeds the organism's growth. Over time, long strands spread out and expand the area of damage. Dry rot consumes the cellulose in the wood, leaving behind material that is shrunken and cracked. The cycle is brought to completion when the fungus produces a fruiting body, a flat, projecting pancake-like growth that produces a new generation of spores.

Certain parts of buildings are particularly vulnerable to dry rot: sills—those low, horizontal timbers laying directly on the foundation—are notorious for rotting. Additionally, wood window and door frames in contact with masonry walls are also liable to this kind of decay. Areas under roof or plumbing leaks are prone to degradation, too.

Some woods are more resistant to rot than others. The favored woods of wooden boat builders perform well: mahogany, white oak, cypress, cedar and certain kinds of pine. Red oak, however, is an especially poor choice. Additionally, wood from the heart, or center of the tree, is more resistant to rot when compared with the sapwood, which is closer to the outside perimeter of a log.

The discovery of dry rot can be alarming, often because it grows in dark, hidden places. It may only be when some other kind of work is being done that deteriorated wood is found. To avoid a repeat of the scenario that brought about the problem to begin with, it is fundamentally important to correct the environmental conditions that contributed to the deterioration.

Using gutters to channel rainwater away from a building's foundation can be helpful. Caulking cracks in walls that might allow water into a structure is also a good idea. And repairing chronic roof or plumbing leaks should also be done.

Once any sources of unwanted moisture have been eliminated, repair of damaged areas can begin. The traditional prescription is to excavate all decayed wood until one has reached solid timber. New wood is then inserted.

However, in specific instances where such replacement would be damaging to historic materials and features, it may be technically possible to leave existing, historic material in place, if the area is truly dry to prevent a new active infestation and if the area is or can be made structurally stable.

The use of pressure-treated or naturally rot-resistant wood is also recommended. New nontoxic treatments employing boron are now available.

By being aware of the causes and effects of dry rot, one can prevent problems before they begin and correct them effectively to help preserve historic buildings for the future.

Air Conditioning in Historic Buildings

Modern climate control systems have both advantages and disadvantages when inserted into historic buildings. By being aware of their effects and taking precautions against their hazards, one can enjoy their benefits while avoiding their liabilities.

Personal comfort, of course, is the primary reason why we like air conditioning. It also tends to be good for the contents of buildings, such as wood furniture, books, textiles, paintings and leather goods—organic materials that would otherwise be subject to decay. Climate control stabilizes the interior environment, keeping humidity and temperature constant while preserving delicate materials.

Unfortunately, air conditioning can be hard on the building itself, leading to moisture problems that can hasten a structure's decay, mostly due to condensation. Consider this analogy: pour a glass of iced tea and place it outside on a hot, humid day. Condensation quickly forms on the outside of the glass, and before long, you have a small puddle of water to mop up. That glass could be your house.

Given this dynamic, when air conditioning buildings, take certain precautions to minimize difficulties. Perhaps most importantly, use air conditioning in moderation. The colder the interior, the more likely moisture problems will manifest themselves. Condensation will appear at any temperature cooler than the dew point. Keeping interior space warmer than a meat locker saves money, too.

The compressor of any air conditioner, whether a central or through the window, will be a magnet for condensing moisture, since it is the coldest element of the unit. Knowing this, make certain that this water has a path away from the building.

Install window units so that no condensation runs toward the building, which over time will result in damage to windowsills and other portions of the building below the window. Water should either dissipate through the fan or drip away from the wall from an outboard corner of the unit. To avoid puddles and algae outside, a tray, pan or funnel together with a hose can carry water away.

Central systems should have insulated ductwork to save energy and to decrease the amount of condensation that would otherwise form and drip into unwanted places, such as ceilings.

Pans underneath ductwork should carry condensation away through both a primary drain and a secondary drain, if needed. Algae often clog these drains, requiring regular maintenance to keep clear.

Insulating buildings provides mixed results. On the plus side, it mediates the difference in temperature between the inside and the outside, preventing the exterior wall from getting so cold: picture that iced tea in a thermos instead of a glass. Many seeking to save energy start by adding insulation in the attic, usually a safe bet.

On the downside, be aware that insulation in certain conditions can create problems of its own, absorbing water and becoming waterlogged without the use of a vapor barrier. A vapor barrier exists to prevent moisture from wicking into and through the structure. Dampness inside the fabric of a building creates a welcome environment for insects such as termites and ants as well as fungus and rot.

And for buildings that are air conditioned and not heated, the vapor barrier goes on the outdoor side of the insulation, not the inside—just the reverse of northern climates.

With these caveats in mind, you can balance the need for preserving your comfort and belongings with that of preserving your old building.

Historic Integrity

While many qualities and features can help make a property historic, integrity emerges as a key, overarching concept in all well-preserved buildings.

The dictionary definition provides some insight: integrity comes from the same root as integrate, suggesting that something is whole, intact, undamaged, unadulterated or "having unreduced or unbroken completeness or totality." A second related meaning implies soundness, coherence, honesty and genuineness resulting from being internally consistent. This characteristic can apply equally to people and objects.

Relating specifically to historic buildings, integrity as defined by the National Register of Historic Places is "the ability of a property to convey its significance." Of course, inanimate objects can only "convey" anything by physical qualities that observers can observe and interpret. Therefore, integrity would seem to be embedded within the fabric of buildings themselves.

The National Register goes on to articulate seven aspects or qualities of integrity: design, materials, workmanship, location, setting, feeling and association. These qualities begin to point toward tangible examples of historic integrity.

Integrity of design is present when a building retains its historic form or has been added to in a way that is consistent with that form.

Integrity of materials results from possessing actual historic fabric; if deterioration has damaged historic materials, new materials are inserted in kind; or if using historic materials is not possible, the new materials have the same visual qualities as the old.

Integrity of workmanship derives from the artisanry involved in creating a building. This includes both the preservation of surviving examples of historic work as well as the practice of high-quality, contemporary craftsmanship that is consistent with historic work.

Integrity of location exists when a building is on its historic site, recognizing that part of its significance comes from where it is.

Integrity of setting is present when a building's historic surroundings remain or have not been altered in such a way to diminish the historic character of the structure.

The last two aspects of integrity are fuzzier:

Integrity of feeling suggests that enough historic features remain to convey the mood of an era.

Integrity of association allows a historic building to show a linkage between surviving materials and past events.

So for example, a building retaining its historic integrity would preserve its historic design and appearance, with new additions skillfully integrated with the old. It would also have a good amount of historic fabric, with matching new materials carefully inserted if necessary. Additionally, it would still be in its historic location with a complementary context. And finally it would continue to convey the aura of and draw a visible connection to the past.

By contrast, a building without historic integrity would be so altered as to be unrecognizable as historic. It would have lost most of its historic materials and would suffer from poor workmanship. It would have been moved or have unsympathetic surroundings. And it would no longer evoke the mood of or suggest any relation to history.

In many cases, the distinction is not nearly so clear-cut. In any given building, certain features may survive in pristine condition, while other elements may be lost. But with an understanding of historic integrity, we can better recognize and maintain surviving historic attributes, while mitigating insensitive changes with work that enhances and reclaims a building's earlier character.

International Preservation Standards

One of the world's most beautiful and historic cities—Venice, Italy—hosted delegates from around the world in 1964 to come to some agreement about the essential principles of historic preservation. Those international representatives, coming from such divergent places as Tunisia, Peru and Poland, grappled with the same multiplicity of questions currently facing people who deal with old buildings.

Preservation is complicated. As soon as one starts examining a historic building and trying to decide what to do with it, a host of questions presents itself: What makes this building historic? What parts of it should we preserve? What parts of it may we alter? What is the significance of its setting? How can we use this building now? What preservation philosophy will guide work on this building?

Struggling with the most basic issues of historic preservation, the Venice delegates bridged their differences to find the common principles that anyone working with historic buildings is likely to face.

Emerging from that discussion is what came to be known as the Venice Charter. This seminal document can be helpful to anyone seeking to understand the essentials of preservation. Moreover, many of its basic ideas overlap with American preservation practice, particularly through "The Secretary of the Interior's Standards for Rehabilitation," forming the basis of preservation guidelines across the country, including the Florida Keys.

In reviewing the Venice Charter, one sees twelve themes:

1. Modest historic buildings that contribute to historic districts are as worthy of preservation as individually important, more elaborate buildings. We should not simply write off small and simple buildings as insignificant.

2. Historic buildings are valuable both aesthetically and as a record of the past. Consequently, solely making buildings "pretty" should not drive preservation efforts.
3. Historic buildings must have modern uses to survive in the future, but there are limits to the changes that can be made to accommodate new functions.
4. New buildings in historic districts should be in scale with their historic neighbors.
5. Part of the significance of historic buildings comes from their location. Consequently, we should not move buildings except to save them from the wrecking ball.
6. Architectural elements have more significance when left in place. Therefore, we should not remove them for salvage, unless the building of which they are a part is destined for demolition.
7. Restoration "must stop at the point where conjecture begins," and new work "must be distinct from" the old "and must bear a contemporary stamp."
8. Buildings usually embody layers of history, which work together to contribute to their significance. As a general rule we should preserve later historic changes as well as remaining original features.
9. Decisions about proposed changes to historic buildings should not "rest solely on the individual in charge of the work."
10. New work should "integrate harmoniously with the original."
11. Additions, if undertaken, should be sensitive to historic buildings and their settings.
12. Records relating to preservation and restoration "should be placed in the archives of a public institution and made available to posterity."

To anyone searching for a basic set of preservation standards, many of these principles strike a resonant chord. They help articulate prime concerns about historic buildings and provide some direction conceptually. Over time, they created a touchstone for preservation efforts worldwide.

The complete text of the Venice Charter can be found on the home page of the International Council on Monuments and Sites: www.international.icomos.org/e_venice.htm

Preservation, Restoration, Rehabilitation: What's The Difference?

Preservation, restoration, rehabilitation: although many terms describe treatments for historic properties, it is helpful to understand the differences between these three, not just as a semantic exercise, but because clarity in understanding reflects clarity in planning and executing work on historic buildings.

Preservation, perhaps the most widely used of these terms, appears frequently in a broad sense, as in *historic preservation*, which defines this entire field of endeavor.

Yet preservation can also describe more specifically the process of keeping as much as possible of the actual historic fabric of a building. Over time, continued attentiveness to the needs of structures exemplifies good stewardship and responsible maintenance, requiring minimal intervention and few, if any, changes. Preservation recognizes the need for in-kind repairs but prevents inappropriate alterations and sweeping redos that would destroy historic features, requiring reinstatement later. Consequently, no dramatic "before" and "after" photographs document pure preservation efforts, which splashy renovations too often overshadow. Well-preserved buildings gradually acquire a patina, an air of antiquity, which really makes them look like old buildings. Indeed, stepping into one can feel like entering a time capsule. Examples of this in the Keys are the Heritage House on Caroline Street, the Oldest House on Duval Street and the Bat Tower on Sugarloaf Key.

Restoration is the process of bringing a building back to a previous appearance in its history. While this is not necessarily its original construction date—it can also be an intermediate date in history—restoration still involves selecting a point in time and seeking to recreate it architecturally. This implies that a building has seen many changes that need to be "undone." A restoration program may call for the removal of inappropriate alterations and poorly conceived additions. Sound documentation, such as historic photographs, building records and evidence in the structure itself, should guide the work. Absent these, restoring with integrity and authenticity requires careful judgment to determine what is appropriate. Without adequate information, it is generally better to leave well enough alone, stopping work where conjecture begins. Pure restoration, inside and out, is often the province of museums seeking the highest standard for their buildings. Examples of successful restoration in the Keys are the Little White House, the Custom House and Pigeon Key.

By far the largest category, rehabilitation involves making a building fit for a contemporary use while still maintaining features that define its historic character. Candidates for this approach often have experienced deterioration and require significant work, usually involving the updating of building systems (plumbing, bathroom and kitchen fixtures, air conditioning), the adding of inconspicuous contemporary features (such as decks and pools) and possibly the construction of new additions. Sometimes, rehabilitation involves a change of use and sensitive alterations to allow the structure to function economically in the modern world. Rehabbed buildings in Key West are the Gato Building at Simonton and Virginia Streets, the Casa Marina, the Tavernier Methodist Church, the Islamorada Library and many Old Town houses.

Once we see preservation, restoration and rehabilitation as separate categories, we can also see how they blend together. In any given building, for example, a much-altered exterior façade may be restored carefully based on a historic photograph. Fine interior detailing and craftsmanship may be preserved as is, and a new addition and utilities may be installed to rehabilitate the structure for contemporary use.

A well-integrated approach to dealing with historic buildings recognizes the complexity of these issues and balances them appropriately to ensure the continuance of the past into the future.

Rehabilitation Guidelines

Many people responsible for historic buildings and faced with the variety of demands they present ask how to approach working on old properties. Those wondering where to begin can turn to the following framework: a suggested, six-step checklist to figuring out what to do next. Based on "The Secretary of the Interior's Standards for Rehabilitation," these recommendations begin with simple measures, progressing in order to more drastic actions.

1. *Identify, Retain, Preserve.* The first task begins with examining what is already there. Perform an inventory of historic features to determine what elements give the building its unique character. Having recognized what is significant, one can then make a conscious effort to leave these features in place. Keep in mind that even the gradual loss of small historic elements may result in a dramatic cumulative effect, compromising a building's overall historic integrity. This conservative approach, emphasizing the status quo, can also help save money by preventing needless alterations that can run up construction costs.

2. *Protect and Maintain.* Once one has decided what elements help define the historic character of a building, the next step is to keep them in good condition. Certain basic tasks are essential for the continued use of historic buildings: caulking, painting, cleaning gutters and removing rust. While such work may not be glamorous, it is a fundamental aspect of taking care of our heritage.

3. *Repair.* Next, those portions of buildings that escaped our best efforts to protect demand our attention. When things break or show signs of deterioration, it is time to fix them—

ideally before they grow to unmanageable proportions. Keep ahead of termites, rot, ultraviolet light and other forms of material degradation. When deterioration requires it, patch areas in poor condition, using the same kind of material if possible. Staying on top of needed repairs is a hallmark of good long-term stewardship. Moreover, buildings under this kind of care will never need to be radically "restored" since they will always be well preserved.

4. *Replace.* If deterioration of an entire feature of a building makes repair impossible, it is appropriate to replace the feature. The new work should follow the historic form exactly, preferably using the same material. Indeed, substitute materials should not be used unless it is technically infeasible to use historic materials. Additionally, substitute materials should have the same visual qualities as the historic materials.

5. *Design for Missing Historic Features.* In some cases, buildings have experienced significant alterations or deterioration, leaving us with the task of filling in the gaps. In recreating these lost elements, we can take two different approaches, depending upon how much evidence remains. If old photographs, surviving documents or physical clues in the building itself point toward an earlier configuration of the structure, it may be possible to replicate historic elements with some fidelity. If, however, the design of a missing historic feature is purely conjectural, it is usually better to create a new design that is compatible with the remaining historic fabric yet differentiated from it. This avoids creating a false sense of historical development.

6. *Alteration and Additions.* This final stage can result in the biggest changes to historic buildings. Consequently, the recommended approach is to avoid jumping to these interventions without due consideration of the alternatives. While it may seem that such changes are necessary, it is usually preferable from a preservation point of view to use the structure as is.

If, however, changes are required to permit an efficient contemporary use, one should design those changes so that the primary character-defining features of the historic

> building are respected and preserved. Alterations and additions should be inconspicuous, harmoniously integrated with the historic building while still discernable as new work.

Keeping these priorities in mind when working with an old building can help guide rehabilitation activities to preserve old buildings' irreplaceable historic qualities for future generations.

For more information regarding the "Standards for Rehabilitation," go to www2.cr.nps.gov/tps/tax/rhb/guide.htm.

Old Buildings, New Uses

While retaining their best attributes, fitting new uses into old buildings is one of the central, recurring challenges of historic preservation. This important issue appears in the very first "Secretary of the Interior's Standards for Rehabilitation," which states: "A property shall be used for its historic purpose or be placed in a new use that requires minimal change to the defining characteristics of the building and its site and environment."

This approach recognizes two options—keeping a historic function or finding a new one—and offers a way to evaluate proposed new uses.

Not surprisingly, continuing the traditional purpose of a structure is usually simpler, since it minimizes the need for substantial design alterations. Fortunately, most historic rehabilitations do not involve a change in use. Houses, for example, by far the largest category of historic buildings, often continue to serve their original function.

Yet sometimes old uses are no longer viable, especially for large, purpose-built structures that outlive their original function, such as warehouses, military buildings and churches. At this point, the second option comes into play: find a new use for the building requiring only "minimal change" to its "defining characteristics."

"Defining characteristics" are those primary features that give a property its special, historic quality, such as materials, spaces, design elements and examples of craftsmanship.

This option can be more challenging because it involves making a judgment concerning what the "defining characteristics" of a building are, and making sure that they experience "minimal change." Yet if one starts with an evaluation of the historic building, appropriate uses may become apparent.

For example, what we now know as the Waterfront Playhouse in Mallory Square historically served as a warehouse and icehouse. Architecturally, its design would seem to constrain other possible uses, since the massive brick structure has no windows, and adding them would have been technically difficult and historically inappropriate. Consequently, the decision to use it as a theater proved providential, since playhouses do not need windows. The new use fits in with virtually no change to essential features of the building.

Another old building nearby, the old Coast Guard headquarters, had some similar challenges, but on a much larger scale. The navy erected this enormous structure on Front Street in the middle of the nineteenth century as the first permanent navy depot on the island. A series of brick buttresses taper out from the sidewalls, supporting a distinctive metal roof. Inside, the volume of space is cavernous. During the 1970s, the government listed the structure as excess property, ultimately paving the way for the commercial use it serves today. As Clinton Square Market, it now houses a set of retail stores in one of the few covered shopping malls in Key West.

The Ley Memorial Chapel on Truman Avenue represents another category of buildings sometimes needing new uses: churches. In this and similar cases, shrinking congregations and consolidating denominations result in empty sanctuaries. Sensitively rehabilitating these distinguished edifices involves recognizing their character-defining interior spaces, stained-glass windows and other unique features. The Ley Chapel successfully accommodated a new office use by employing interior partitions to create cubicles instead of full-height walls to enclose rooms. As a result, the soaring interior space is still plainly visible, and the Wesley House Community Center enjoys a distinctive new headquarters.

Although it is important that new uses fit appropriately in historic buildings, historic preservation commissions generally do not have the power to regulate the function of historic buildings. They review design and appearance only.

Regulating the use of buildings instead falls on other government agencies. For example, planning boards regulate categories of use in particular neighborhoods through zoning. Moreover, state and local licensing laws, although not usually specifically written to encourage historic preservation, provide additional controls over such uses as hotels, bars and restaurants.

Determining appropriate uses for old buildings ultimately derives from a combination of design considerations, economic concerns and regulatory issues. By bearing in mind those special features that define the character of historic buildings—and minimizing the change done to them—old buildings can house new uses, allowing them to pay their way economically while still retaining the significant qualities that make them historic.

Preserving Historic Changes

Retaining later alterations to structures may seem contrary to one of the traditional goals of historic preservation: restoration of original features. However, restoration is not the only option, and it is not always the best.

Standard Four of "The Secretary of the Interior's Standards for Rehabilitation" may offer some guidance: "Most properties change over time; those changes that have acquired historic significance in their own right shall be retained and preserved."

Early advocates for historic preservation gave priority to restoration, removing later work and replacing missing earlier work to recreate the form of a property at a particular time. For example, restorers in nineteenth-century Europe removed newer work from medieval cathedrals—this on a continent where the definition of "new" is very broad. (New College at Oxford University was founded in 1379.) They scraped off later plaster and took out other additions, provoking debate with opponents who decried the removal of material that was still historic, even if it was not original. The ensuing argument between "scrape" and "anti-scrape" parties would continue to have resonance in later generations.

During the 1930s, John D. Rockefeller Jr. began restoring the colonial capital of Williamsburg, Virginia, gradually acquiring most properties in that historic district and tearing down all buildings erected after 1776. Restoration proceeded according to high standards of scholarship, but the result garners mixed reviews today. Some appreciate the effort to recreate a specific moment in time, while others say the effect appears phony: an artificial colonial theme park with two centuries of intervening history erased from the landscape.

Deciding which elements to preserve and which to remove consequently hinges on the interpretation of "changes that have acquired historic significance in their own right." Some criteria to follow include age, defensibility over time and period of significance (for the property's history, architecture and occupants).

Sheer age, not surprisingly, is a core principle in defining what is historic. In general, to be eligible for the National Register of Historic Places, a resource must be over fifty years old. This is a good rule of thumb, but it does not settle the matter.

The historical period of significance of a building or district also plays a role in determining the value of later work. In the Key West Historic District, for example, old buildings date from the 1830s to the 1930s, with a particularly strong representation of structures from 1886 to 1912. Consequently, changes made during this era are generally worth preserving.

Architectural significance is another quality to consider. Some changes become an integral part of the history of a building, testifying to its evolution over time and serving as representative examples of craftsmanship or building technique. For example, many old houses in Key West have later (but still historic) kitchen wings embodying the need for utilitarian service areas. At the same time, other additions may obscure primary features defining a building's character. The Wesley House Community Center rightly restored the old Ley Chapel on Truman Avenue, removing a 1960s concrete block façade that masked the earlier form and appearance of the building.

Preserving a building as an earlier occupant would remember can also suggest the value of historic changes. Restoring the Hemingway House to its original 1860s appearance would wipe out material relating to the writer's residency there in the 1930s. Likewise, bringing the Harry S. Truman Little White House back to its earlier form as built in the 1890s would destroy evidence of its presidential history in the forties and fifties. Consequently, these buildings show several layers of history.

Finally, when making the decision to take away later additions, we might ask whether the removal is an act for which later generations will thank or criticize us, as we are stewards of these properties for our tenure only. The buildings will outlive us, and what we do to them will have an impact after we are gone.

By being sensitive to these concerns, we can preserve not just single moments in the tangible remains of the past, but also the multi-generational, many-layered, evolutionary character of history.

Additions and New Construction

Inserting new work into historic contexts—such as new additions to historic buildings or entirely new structures in historic districts—involves a careful balancing act between two opposites: making the new work indistinguishable from the old or making it stand out too much.

Standard Nine of "The Secretary of the Interior's Standards for Rehabilitation" recognizes this paradox:

"The new work shall be differentiated from the old and shall be compatible with the massing, size, scale and architectural features to protect the historic integrity of the property and its environment."

Most people are not surprised to learn that new work should be "compatible" with its historic context, since so much of the modern historic preservation movement sprung from a rebellion against ugly, modern, out-of-scale and otherwise incompatible new construction during the 1950s and '60s. At that time, the need for sensitively integrated new construction was painfully obvious.

The idea that new work should also be differentiated from the old may seem counterintuitive. Some observers might think it best to integrate new work seamlessly with the old, so that one does not even know that new work is new.

Yet a couple of compelling reasons militate against this. First, blurring the lines between old and new can cause confusion, diminishing the integrity and authenticity of genuine historic buildings. Without some distinction between the contributions of different periods, original properties can get lost in new work. Second, new architecture does not need to completely surrender its identity just because it is in a historic context. It, too, is a product of its time, worthy of recognition for honestly expressing that.

During the last thirty years, ideas about what is an appropriate balance between compatibility and differentiation have changed. The distinction does not need to be as obvious now, as subtle cues marking new work are considered sufficient. The evolution in interpreting this concept is evident in the Casa Marina, where a 1970s addition on Seminole Avenue is obviously modern, while a later wing on Reynolds Street blends in better.

Ensuring that new work is both "differentiated from" and "compatible with" the old involves paying close attention to "the massing, size, scale and architectural features" that Standard Nine mentions.

Massing refers to shape and form. The first consideration governing this is location: where on a site the new work will go. Generally, additions to existing historic buildings should be to the rear or on an inconspicuous side elevation, while new buildings in a historic district should maintain the setbacks of the neighborhood.

Another aspect to massing is the actual form of the structure. The best additions quietly echo the massing of the original building, sometimes having only a minimal link to it, such as a "hyphen" or connecting corridor. The addition to the Monroe County courthouse exemplifies this. Likewise, successful new construction in historic districts will pick up the traditional shapes of surrounding buildings, such as roof forms.

Size and scale refer to sheer volume (length, width and height), especially in relation to context. It is extremely difficult for new work that is too big to be compatible with its surroundings. At the same time, appropriately scaled new work has a fighting chance of fitting in.

Architectural features include siding, roofing, windows, doors and decoration. These elements provide opportunities to carefully pick up some details while at the same time using differences to set the new apart from the old.

Notable examples demonstrating all these qualities include a new house at 701 Elizabeth Street on Solares Hill, occupying a small, odd-shaped corner lot. The structure is clearly new, while still harmonizing with—and not upstaging—its historic residential neighbors. Another corner property, Wachovia Bank, features a new addition on Duval Street. Terra cotta colors and decorative cornices relate to the main building; still, the glorious brickwork, balcony and turret on the historic Moorish Revival style bank are left to shine without competition.

Common Mistakes in Rehabbing

Although countless rehabilitations of historic properties take place each year, presenting a myriad of unique challenges and difficulties, pitfalls usually appear in only a few categories. To steer clear of trouble and learn from the mistakes of others (rather than your own), here is a list of problems to avoid, a baker's half dozen of all-too-common treatments that can compromise the integrity of historic buildings:

1. *Removing too much historic fabric.* Although deterioration may require the replacement of some historic material, care should be taken to retain as much as possible. Otherwise, a project that started out as rehabilitation can turn into new construction. Without appreciable genuine material from the past, old buildings risk losing their integrity, since the tangible remains of history give them their authenticity. Consequently, respecting historic fabric is the first principle of historic preservation.

2. *Removing elements from a building that are not original to its construction—even though they are genuinely historic.* This often occurs by overstressing restoration at the expense of preservation. While it may seem odd to criticize restoration, a sole focus on returning a structure to its earliest appearance may result in the loss of historic material from other, more recent periods in its history. Indeed, buildings frequently embody qualities from more than one era. Respecting and preserving other chapters—not just the first—in a building's history allow it to tell its whole story.

3. *Creating additions that are indistinguishable as new work.* While some people may point with pride to a new addition blending seamlessly into an historic building, this can affect the property's design integrity, causing confusion as to which parts are old or new. An observer should be able to read the evolution of a building in order to see how it grew and changed over the years. We should also design and construct additions so that future generations can remove them while still leaving the earlier building unimpaired. In this way, an "addition" can become a "subtraction" without doing lasting damage.

4. *Decorating buildings to be more ornate than they were historically.* Many old buildings are straightforward, vernacular structures, often relying on their simplicity and good proportions for their appeal. Yet some people want them to be more high-style than they are, tarting them up with fancy doorways, fake gingerbread or extra moldings and trimmings. This embellishment can obscure good qualities and create a false impression of how a building looked. To avoid this pitfall, let the modest designs of the past stand with simple grace and unimpaired dignity.

5. *Trying to accommodate an incompatible use into a building that was designed for a very different use.* Adapting old properties for new purposes is a much heralded strategy for historic preservation, but sometimes the gap between the container and the contained is too wide. Not attempting to force a square peg into a round hole can prevent these awkward adaptations.

6. *Failing to use the gentlest means possible for cleaning, stripping and refinishing.* Sandblasting can strip away the outer, glazed surfaces of bricks and can cause deep indentations and channels on wood surfaces. Even pressure washing that is over six hundred PSI can damage wood. Remember the Hippocratic Oath: do no harm.

7. *Trying to slog through complicated design and rehabilitation projects without adequate professional help.* Historic preservation is both an art and a science, involving many different fields of expertise: history, architecture, engineering, carpentry and masonry. Large projects require experienced people who

understand design, construction, codes, decoration, crafts and trades. Failing to use knowledgeable people can result in poor work quality and the need to redo inadequate jobs. Hire professionals to do the work.

By keeping these potential pitfalls in mind, one can avoid problems that have ensnared others, allowing rehabilitation projects to proceed successfully, preserving the irreplaceable qualities of historic buildings for future generations to enjoy.

Preserving the Recent Past

How old is historic?

Answering this question involves making a distinction, separating those buildings and sites that are notable and worthy of preservation from those that are not.

One's perspective—such as geographic and cultural background—certainly can play a role:

Europeans, for example, may look at the United States with mild amusement, since everything over here is so "new." Compared to ancient, medieval and Renaissance architecture abroad, that may be true.

Even within our own country, those from the original thirteen colonies have long treasured their colonial and Revolutionary past, an emphasis that led them only slowly to appreciate Victorian and later periods.

The Old South has a dynamic all its own, traditionally looking back romantically to the antebellum era, while de-emphasizing later times.

Here in Key West, the Golden Age according to long tradition was the nineteenth century: the age of wreckers, sea captains and merchants. This has led some to downplay anything that is not Victorian.

In addition to these cultural factors, one's longevity also may influence one's perception of what is historic. Older people may discount resources from decades still within their memory, while younger people may have an interest in those same times, which may date from before they were born. To twenty-somethings, the 1950s and '60s may seem retro and hip.

In the eyes of American law (in the form of the National Historic Preservation Act) resources older than fifty years old may be eligible for inclusion in the National Register of Historic Places.

The act does not automatically disqualify resources fewer than fifty years old from listing, but the standard is higher and the burden of proof shifts. Younger resources must be of exceptional significance, and sound scholarship should bolster the case.

Here in Key West, we can see an expansion in the definition of what is historic through the evolution of the historic district. As defined in the 1960s, the earliest area excluded much of the waterfront and extended southeast only to Angela Street. Subsequent efforts added Truman Annex, the Meadows and the neighborhoods beyond the cemetery to the Casa Marina.

Moreover, the Key West Bight was also not originally part of the historic district, which stopped at Caroline Street. Later the Thompson Fish House, Turtle Kraals and Cannery saw inclusion in the National Register of Historic Places, and the local district expanded as well. Now, the City has renamed the area the "Historic Seaport," showing a new appreciation for its significance—understandable in light of the now-extinct shrimp boat era that flourished there during the 1950s.

More recently, the City has added properties outside the contiguous historic district to the inventory of historic buildings in Key West. These include the early twentieth-century cigar factory at Staples Avenue and Second Street, along with nearby houses featuring ornamental concrete block. Other structures beyond Old Town stand on Eagle Avenue, displaying 1920s Mediterranean Revival elements such as red tile roofs and stucco walls.

Up in Tavernier, fieldwork in the 1980s turned up a couple dozen potentially historic buildings. A more recent effort found fifty to sixty, and many more may become eligible for inclusion in the next few years.

Further afield, one can find examples of newly recognized historic places around the country: the Levittowns built immediately following World War II, the first McDonald's fast-food restaurant and such icons of modernism as the Lever House in New York City, the Farnsworth House in Illinois and Philip Johnson's Glass House in Connecticut.

Evaluating the recent past is the cutting edge of preservation and probably always will be. Most everyone agrees that we should preserve the very old: the rarest and most valuable surviving materials. Yet those resources that date from within a human lifetime can provoke discussion and even controversy.

For those looking to the past for a fixed canon that provides stability, the need to reevaluate what is historic can cause unease. Yet the definition of historic is clearly a moving target: we are continually advancing into the future, and those resources not lost to the ravages of time continue to grow older and take on new significance.

Appendix

"The Secretary of the Interior's Standards for Rehabilitation":

1. A property shall be used for its historic purpose or be placed in a new use that requires minimal change to the defining characteristics of the building and its site and environment.

2. The historic character of a property shall be retained and preserved. The removal of historic materials or alteration of features and spaces that characterize a property shall be avoided.

3. Each property shall be recognized as a physical record of its time, place and use. Changes that create a false sense of historical development, such as adding conjectural features or architectural elements from other buildings, shall not be undertaken.

4. Most properties change over time; those changes that have acquired historic significance in their own right shall be retained and preserved.

5. Distinctive features, finishes and construction techniques or examples of craftsmanship that characterize a historic property shall be preserved.

6. Deteriorated historic finishes shall be repaired rather than replaced. Where the severity of deterioration requires replacement of a distinctive feature, the new feature shall match the old in design, color, texture and other visual qualities and where possible, materials. Replacement of missing features shall be substantiated by documentary, physical or pictorial evidence.

7. Chemical or physical treatments, such as sandblasting, that cause damage to historic materials shall not be used. The surface cleaning of structures, if appropriate, shall be undertaken using the gentlest means possible.

8. Significant archaeological resources affected by a project shall be protected and preserved. If such resources must be disturbed, mitigation measures shall be undertaken.

9. New additions, exterior alterations or related new construction shall not destroy historic materials that characterize the property. The new work shall be differentiated from the old and shall be compatible with the massing, size, scale and architectural features to protect the historic integrity of the property and its environment.

10. New additions and adjacent or related new construction shall be undertaken in such a manner that if removed in the future, the essential form and integrity of the historic property and its environment would be unimpaired.